The Six Traits of Self-Leadership

How to Create a Life of Success and Happiness

2018

The Six Traits of Self-Leadership

How to Create a Life of Success and Happiness

First Edition: May 2018

ISBN 978-1-908293-46-6

© Michael Daly 2018

Michael Daly has asserted his rights under the Copyright, Designs and Patents act 1988 to be identified as the author of this work.

All rights reserved in all media. This book may not be copied, stored, transmitted or reproduced in any format or medium without specific prior permission from the authors or publisher.

Published by:

CGW Publishing
B 1502
PO Box 15113
Birmingham
B2 2NJ
United Kingdom

www.cgwpublishing.com

mail@cgwpublishing.com

To learn more about The Six Traits of Self-Leadership, visit

www.michaeldalyireland.com

michael@michaeldalyireland.com

For my mother, Mary and my late father, John.

Contents

Foreword..10

Preface..14

Introduction..18
   A personal belief...22
   Having a practical and grounded perspective......26
   Start where you are...27

Trait 1 Being Determined....................................30
   Step up to the challenge....................................32
   The joy of overcoming problems........................34
   Turn to face your fears.......................................37
   Do you play it safe or do you take risks?...........39
   How do you view failure?..................................41
   Ever the optimist..47
   Where you are now..48

Trait 2 Getting Creative.......................................52
   How creative do you think you are?...................58
   Invest in your creativity.....................................60
   Harnessing your creativity.................................65
   Where you are now..68

Trait 3 Playing to your Strengths.......................72
   What is meant by a 'personal strength'?............75
   Being true to yourself..77
   Putting your strengths to work...........................78
   What is meant by a 'personal weakness'?.........82
   Identifying your weaknesses.............................84
   Staying alert..88
   Where you are now..92

Trait 4 Having a Vision for your Life and Work..........96
    Having a vision..........100
    Your vision..........102
    Describing your vision..........104
    Defining your vision..........107
    Believe in your vision..........111
    Right now is all you have..........113
    Where you are now..........114

Trait 5 Knowing your Mission..........118
    The mission statement..........121
    Setting meaningful goals..........123
    Achieving your goals..........128
    Where you are now..........137

Trait 6 Staying Focused..........142
    Focusing on your vision..........145
    Knowing when to say yes and when to say no..........147
    Weekly planning..........150
    Compromise and balance are not always the answer..........156
    Where you are now..........158

Conclusion..........162
    Never ever give in..........165
    Where you are now..........167

Acknowledgements..........172

About The Author..........178

Praise for The Six Traits of Self-Leadership: How to Create a Life of Success and Happiness.

Some public-spirited individual ought to send this book to Leo Varadkar.

Gene Kerrigan, Journalist and Author – Ireland

One of the smartest books you will ever read.

Professor Jim Blythe, Cardiff – Wales

I recently experienced two moments of enlightenment – listening to Michael's lectures and reading his book on self-leadership. A simplicity of recommendations leading to peace between your mind and heart, a clear vision of your own life and encouragement to immediately turn your thoughts to the inner belief that "everything is going to work out just right"! You cannot remain at the same stage of your life journey as you were before opening the first pages of this book.

Jolanta Preidiene, Head of International Department, Vilnius University of Applied Sciences – Lithuania

This book is both moving and practical. It also reflects the personal experience of the author – a self-leader I admire and respect. It is a fantastic read and gives exceptional every-day-life examples for the reader to put straight into practice. This is a book that will make an impact and it is a must read. So, let it act as your personal assistant and manual as you create a life of success and happiness for The Six Traits of Self-Leadership shows you how.

Professor María José Del Pino Espejo, University Pablo de Olavide, Seville – Spain

If you read one book this year, make it this one – it has it all. It will show how you can bring success and happiness to your life and work so as to truly live the life you want to have.

Nick Williams, internationally acclaimed author and inspired entrepreneur – London, England

The Six Traits of Self-Leadership is an excellent book, which I highly recommend to anyone who wants to achieve their personal and professional goals. It provides a simple approach to success and happiness, something most of us want. It reveals the Six Traits that will make you more effective. This book is easy to follow and very inspiring. One of the most powerful and insightful books I've ever read!

Professor Ana Paula Lopes, University of Oporto – Portugal

Michael Daly has given us an outstanding prescription for getting the kind of satisfaction we want from our lives. In his book The Six Traits of Self-Leadership: How to Create a Life of Success and Happiness, he has shown how satisfaction is not just about some outsider telling us what to do but really about self-leadership, the way to real personal happiness.

Michael gives us the keys to self-leadership with his six traits and illustrates each with down-to-earth examples. The ideas are easily accessible and presented in a friendly style that anyone can understand.

Professor Alan Zimmerman, City University of New York – USA

Have you ever asked the question "What do I need to be successful?" The answer is – healthy self-confidence – calmness – and awareness.

You achieve self-confidence through Bildung. Bildung is translated literally as "higher education". Bildung is what's left over when you subtract your lessons learned from your knowledge. Bildung is active! Bildung is not a customer relationship. It is not edutainment or a passive education where you learn a lot. It's all up to you! Calmness means: Don't go charging in. Lay back, think for a while before you act. One night is all it takes.

Be aware. Look into the eyes of your partners. Do they understand your message? In order to understand more, read this book!

Professor. Dr.-Ing. Gerd Mühlenbeck, Heidelberg – Germany

The Six Traits of Self-Leadership makes for great reading. It will inspire readers to reach their full potential in life, regardless of age, education or profession. The style is easy and personal. Not only does the author make a valuable synthesis of ideas from different fields including psychology, time management and entrepreneurship – but he also gives readers advice from his own experience or that of his clients.

The book is practical, filled with inspiring thoughts and quotes, written with determination, passion and a sense of humor.

Dr. Anda Gheorghiu, Associate Professor, Hyperion University Bucharest & Internal Auditor, Romanian National Ombudsman – Romania

Foreword

To be in hell is to drift; to be in heaven is to steer.

George Bernard Shaw

I believe that one of the scarcest resources in the world today is inspired and inspiring leadership. What the world is hungry for is men and women who stand up for the greater good, stand up for what they believe in. What is even more amazing is that we each have leadership within us. We are generally encouraged and programmed to be compliant and follow rules rather than follow our own principles and listen to our inner voice and guidance. We need to shift our thinking from "Dear God, please send me an inspiring leader," to "Dear God, please help me step into my own inspiring leadership." More of us are waking up to the fact that we ourselves are the ones we have been waiting for.

We all have love and leadership gifts in us right now, just waiting to be recognised and shared.

All leadership starts with self-leadership, following your own inspiration and leading your life by your own principles.

The small, still voice that resides within all of us is inviting us to live our own true and precious life. The more aligned we are with our own values, the happier we are, and we automatically start to become an inspiration to others. As you create your own true life, you'll automatically become a leader, not because you'll want others to follow your rules, but because they'll want to follow your example.

When I first met Michael on the Greek island of Skyros over fifteen years ago, he was working as an employee and feeling restless. He sensed that there was a bigger life beckoning him, a new chapter of his own leadership to step into. He was already providing leadership and he was also overdue a new beginning. Since we first met, it has been a pleasure to witness Michael finding the courage to change and follow even more of his own calling. He has had to go against his own programming and expectations to find and live his own true life. I have now made dozens of trips to Ireland and it has been a delight to watch and participate in Michael's growth and see the impact he has made. He left his job to start his own business and do further studies. Michael now teaches internationally; he has transformed himself and his own life and continues to do so.

Michael is now a leader in his own right, a true friend and an inspiration. This book is his gift to you to help you find your own true life. He encourages you to step into your own self-leadership for your own happiness and success and to act as an inspiration to others.

Thank you, Michael.

Nick Williams, London

Preface

May you live all the days of your life.

Jonathan Swift

The book you now hold in your hands started as an article I wrote for an international university publication. It was an article on setting out to live a more successful and happier life. This is an area I personally am passionate about: how best to assist and support individuals to reach their full potential so as to have a more successful and happier life. It is my experience that those who achieve their best and have success and happiness, do so because they do not allow their past to hold them back; nor do they spend their days dreaming about a better future. They take ownership of their present situation, accept where it is they are in life, and then take the time and invest the energy in setting out where it is they want their life to be. In doing so, they show the hallmark of being a self-leader within their own life. Only they now go further and live the life of a self-leader – taking the action necessary to see the future they want for their life actually become a reality.

Having read the initial article, many readers wanted me to go into more detail and flesh out the idea of how living a life of self-leadership leads to having a successful and happy life. So I wrote this book following the simple rules of avoiding referring to anything that I have not witnessed personally, and focusing on each area of self-leadership independently. My aim was to keep it simple, straightforward, to the point and practical at all times.

Many people often wait to be hit between the eyes – to have that moment of clarity about the life they need to live for it to be a happier and more successful one. Yet, it rarely works that way. The reality is that it usually takes years of trying and failing and trying again: lots of ups and downs and not quite getting it right, but feeling closer and closer, warmer and warmer, to the life you want to live. Self-leadership is about going for it, facing the challenges with courage and determination, taking the disappointments with a sense of humour, hanging in there when the going gets tough and never giving up the thought that you will get there in the end, for you surely will.

What would it actually mean to you to live a life of self-leadership? Do you think your life would change for the better? I urge you to read this book and find out just how much better your life could be. Are you ready? Let's start.

Michael E. Daly, Dublin

Please note: Most of the case studies included in this book are based on actual people, but a few have had name changes for the purposes of confidentiality and a couple are an amalgam of several real people.

Introduction

Whatever you can do, or dream you can, begin it now.

Boldness has genius, power and magic in it.

Johann Wolfgang von Goethe

When you hear the word 'leadership', what's the first thing that comes into your mind? Most people think of management, power, position or something that you are born to do. When asked to name leaders they admire, most people think of, for example, Nelson Mandela, Mahatma Gandhi and Bill Clinton. While they may be leaders in their own right, this is neither the type of leader nor the type of leadership that we are referring to here. The leadership we are talking about is one starting with a small 'l' not a big 'L', in the sense of what the traditional definition of a leader is.

Self-leadership begins with you as an individual and your willingness to improve your life. There's no need for big or grandiose achievements. While these may happen, they don't have to for you to live a life of self-leadership. Becoming a self-leader doesn't mean you have to set out to save the world or anything like that. What is meant is that you identify what you love and want to do in life. Having done this, you then give it your all to make these things happen, to take ownership and the responsibility to see that they become an integral part of everything you do as you move forward with your life.

Luck favours the brave and, if you want to live the life of a self-leader, you will need some element of luck, but you will also need to be brave and determined. The fact is, luck often only comes to those who do the legwork, the ones who are prepared to put the time, effort and energy into looking at where they want to be in their life and how best to make this a reality. They are the ones who have the determination to go on and take action to make sure they have a chance of achieving the life they want to live.

They understand that they must take on the traits of the self-leader within their life and work if they are to succeed and be successful.

How many people are just going through the motions of day to day living, reliving the same week over and over again? Indeed, for many people nowadays, it is not only a matter of going through the motions: it is a case of hanging in there and getting through each day, living day to day. People speak in terms of success being about survival, both personally and professionally.

> People end up watching the same programmes on television, making the same daily journey(s), doing the same things day in, day out. They build their lives around the schedules they have for their work (that is, if they have work to go to), home and sleep. They keep their head down and get on with it without allowing themselves time to break out of the daily cycle of their lives.
>
> This gives them no time to think or work towards having a better and brighter future for themselves, their family and their community.
>
> Is this the case for you? Honestly, are you one of those people going through the motions of day to day living, reliving the same week over and over? Or are you just hanging in there, getting through each day, living day to day?

> Many people are in this situation, but it doesn't have to be like that. It is my belief that each and every person can live a life of success and happiness, regardless of their past or the life they are living right now. While they may never have taken the time to think about what they want and why they want it, that does not mean it has to be this way.

Would you like to:

- Live a more fulfilled, contented and successful life?
- Learn how to re-invent or re-engineer your life and work?
- Foster wise decision making within your life and work?
- Give yourself the opportunity to have the focus to live life with clarity and direction in pursuit of the life you want to live?
- Draw up the goals to be achieved to have such a life?
- Have the means to move forward and take the action to see you're living a life of success and happiness?

If you answered 'Yes' to at least one of these questions, then keep reading. By the time you have finished this book, you will have the tools to do all of these things.

A Personal Belief

My interest in living a life of self-leadership is not purely a professional one. It reflects both a personal and professional search to find focus, clarity and direction within my own life and work. It is an attempt to understand why some people have managed to do this while so many others haven't. It was this searching out and understanding why it is that these people have been able to live a more successful and happier life that led me to write this book. The common denominator was that they were living a life of self-leadership. This life of self-leadership involves six common traits that I will now share with you. I will show you how you, too, can live out the six traits within your own life and work in pursuit of a happier and more successful future for yourself and everyone you come into contact with.

When I finished school, I trained to be a monk. While much of this time was dedicated to studying, I also got to work and live with some of the most marginalised and disadvantaged of people and communities. After eight years of studying, it was time for me to either take final monastic vows for life or move on. I chose to move on. I did so because it was as if life was calling me in another direction. It was as if I was meant to be there for the eight years; I learned what was to be learned about myself, people and life while there and then it was time to take my life in a different direction. The world was now opening up new challenges and opportunities to learn and grow as a person, both personally and professionally.

After leaving the monks, my work was initially with young people and involved getting them to take ownership of their own lives and destinies. This work led to me being offered and taking up a management position. This new role had me working with adults, committees, communities, groups and organisations to create a better future for both themselves and all those with whom they came into contact. After a number of years of doing this, it was time for me to move on once again. For the last fifteen years I have been a freelance training consultant (apart from three year-long periods where I took on in-house management roles with organisations for which I had previously acted as a consultant).

Throughout all this time and with all those that my work and life has brought me into contact with, there is one common denominator among those who have achieved or are in the process of achieving success and happiness, both personally and professionally. That is, that they have taken on a role of self-leadership within their life and work. For them, living a life of self-leadership has meant living a life of focus, clarity and direction in pursuit of a happier and more successful future. This book identifies the six traits of self-leadership. If incorporated into your life and work, they will make you both more successful and happier.

The six traits are:

Trait 1: Being Determined

Trait 2: Getting Creative

Trait 3: Playing to your Strengths

Trait 4: Having a Vision for your Life and Work

Trait 5: Knowing your Mission

Trait 6: Staying Focused

EXERCISE

Now take some time to answer the following question:

Which leaders do you admire?

Now remember, these don't have to be leaders with a capital 'L'. They might be leaders that you know that the rest of us don't know. They might come from the world of your work, be teachers or lecturers that you may have had, part of a youth club or sports group you were involved in when growing up, a family member or a charity that you are connected to.

What are the qualities and/or skills that you admire in them?

There are many people living a life of self-leadership. They are not often written about but they do exist. One such person is Anne McFadden. I became friends with Anne while in college in the late 1980s and we have stayed friends ever since. She started out in her career working with some of the most disadvantaged young men and women in Dublin, always giving her best to make their lives better. She worked with them so they would have some hope in their lives.

After moving to Sydney in 1997, she started, once again putting her many skills and talents at the disposal of others. Now, as well as having a full-time job fundraising for cancer research, she is also engaged in supporting the Irish community in Australia. She has been the President of the Sydney St. Patrick's Day Parade and family day on three separate occasions. During her three terms as President, she took it from an under-performing and debt-ridden event to an 'over-performing' one, making a profit on all occasions. (All my own words – Anne would be too modest to say so.)

What I admire about her is:

1. She is a person of determination, focus, conviction and action.

2. She is honest and straight – you will always know where you stand with her.

3. She is a genuinely caring person and one of great humility.

Remember, it is often the same qualities and/or skills that you admire in these leaders that you most need to draw on from within yourself to live your life as a self-leader. It is also frequently the case that what we see in others we have in ourselves – we often just need to nurture and develop these traits.

HAVING A PRACTICAL AND GROUNDED PERSPECTIVE

The aim of this book is to set out a framework and guide you in how best to live a life of self-leadership, which will mean a successful and happier life for you and everyone with whom you come into contact. Understanding and taking ownership within your own life of the six traits discussed in this book will substantially increase the chances of you being happier and more successful. After finishing the book, like all self-leaders, you, too, will have a vision that acts as your personal North Star, a guiding light, around which all decisions will be made to move your life forward to where you want it to be.

When doing the exercises set out, you will have to think and think hard, but not to excess. You will be encouraged, challenged and supported to think constructively. If you find the world won't work the way you want it to – if you can't make things happen despite your very best efforts – by understanding the six traits, you will be assisted in how to change the way you look at the world, thus making things happen for you. This book is about equipping you with the understanding and direction required to drive you forward so you can start right now.

It is normal to question one's life and perhaps decide that changes are required, but there is a risk that this questioning can carry over into a non-productive habit – the habit of excessive thinking. This is a mistake many people tend to make when beginning to work on themselves, like undertaking to read this book. This work is not designed for you to think about yourself excessively. It is designed for you to take the time to reflect on your life and how it is you can make it a happier and more successful one by nurturing and developing the traits of the self-leader within you. It will show you how to then take the necessary action to enable you to have a happier and more successful life.

Start where you are

Self-leaders do not confuse living in the now with living in the future. They always remain hopeful for the future but here, today, is where their life is taking place. They don't dwell on the past, as there is a need to remain hopeful for the future, only it is now where they live life to the best of their ability. They live in the here and now and, at the same time, make real and positive decisions that will bring them forward.

Robert Louis Stevenson once wrote that a successful life is not achieved by being dealt a good hand, but rather by playing a poor hand well. You cannot begin by asking for the deck to be reshuffled, nor will complaints about the dealer get you very far. You must become the dealer in your life, so let us begin.

28

TRAIT 1
BEING DETERMINED

Nobody made a greater mistake than he who did nothing because he could do only a little.

Edmund Burke

When I think of being determined, the acclaimed author and founder of the Inspired Entrepreneur Club, Nick Williams, comes to mind. He really is a great role model when it comes to determination. This is because he is determined to do the work he believes he was born to do regardless of the challenges involved – and there have been many.

Nick walked away from a very 'successful' and highly financially rewarding career selling computers in the 1980s, to help people move beyond their fears, encouraging them to play a bigger part in their own lives and turn their passions into profitable businesses.

Having written seven books and travelled the world to spread his message, he truly is determined to challenge people and show them another way of living than that of the accepted beliefs of society when it comes to work and how to do business.

Whether or not you follow the life you want to live, it won't be easy either way, so why not just go for it? At least then, through all the struggles and strife, it will be in pursuit of what matters most to you as a person. Living a life of self-leadership is not easy – far from it. It is tough, requiring determination and great effort on your part to keep moving forward if you want to live a life of success and happiness.

EXERCISE

Take a moment to think of a time when you had to show real determination in your own life so as to not give in or give up; a time when you had to dig deep within yourself so as to keep moving forward in your life. Maybe it was when you lost a job, the ending of a relationship, a business venture failed or you faced health issues.

Think also of a time when you had to show real determination to achieve something that you wanted in your life. A time when you were determined to get a job, hold onto a job, see a new business venture succeed, deal with an addiction or achieve any personal or professional goal.

Showing determination, either in the face of adversity or in pursuit of something meaningful, is the first trait of a self-leader.

STEP UP TO THE CHALLENGE

Remember that wanting to bring your life and work to a better place in the future, will mean having to deal with and overcome the many problems, challenges and demands that will inevitably arise. Many people have the false belief that as they achieve success, they will be faced with fewer problems.

In fact, it is often the opposite. There are always challenges and problems to overcome in life and work. The challenges and problems will just be in direct proportion to the level of success and happiness you want in life.

There will be times when you will be tempted to give in, believing the challenges and problems to be dealt with are simply too much for you. This is often precisely when there is a need to rise to the occasion. Those who really want success and happiness have the persistence and determination to keep moving forward in pursuit of the life they want, regardless of the challenges and problems that face them.

Self-leaders tend not to dwell on the negative and always look to see the benefits of the situation. The past is not going to invent their future, as this is something they will not entertain. They find a way to move on and create their future; they always find a way to move on, regardless of the circumstances they find themselves in.

When things are not going their way and the whole world seems to be against them, they:

A) accept that they will experience both positive and negative emotions, but they keep moving towards the life they want to live;

B) trust in their abilities and know they can learn from their mistakes as well as their successes;

C) follow their instincts, rather than being influenced by the opinions of others.

The Joy of Overcoming Problems

Now take a moment to identify the last difficulty or problem you had to deal with. Perhaps you couldn't pay a bill, or make a decision whether to accept or reject an invitation, or you felt let down by someone and didn't know what to do about it and so on.

How did you deal with it?

- Did you deal with it head on?
- Did you do nothing in the hope that it would go away?
- Did you get busy so you didn't have to think about it?
- Perhaps you hoped someone else would come along and solve it for you.
- Maybe you sought out advice and assistance so you could deal with it.

Next, please go one step further and name the difficulty or problem you have to deal with in your life at this time. Which option from the above would best assist you in overcoming this problem or difficulty? Regardless of the difficulties or problems you are now facing, please keep in mind the serenity prayer by Karl Paul Reinhold Niebuhr:

God, give us grace to accept with serenity the things that cannot be changed, courage to change the things that should be changed, and wisdom to distinguish the one from the other.

Self-leaders recognise and accept the fact that overcoming difficulties and problems successfully does lead to a greater sense of fulfilment. They know that this makes them stronger, ready for the next challenge and whatever difficulties or problems life will present. Sooner or later, most people learn that the future is not determined so much by what happens to them. Who they are and what they become will be decided predominantly by how they respond to the difficulties that confront them.

It will just not be possible to plan for every possible difficulty or problem that may arise in the future.

Trying to second guess everything that may or may not happen in the future will cripple your ability to stay centred and act in the moment. The here and now is all you have and it really is the only point of power you can truly operate from.

You can only overcome difficulties and solve problems if and when they happen.

It is often natural for human beings to want the easy way out. This may seem the best way. It is so much easier to fit in and not stand out, just keep our head down and get on with it. Not bringing any attention to ourselves, as this might aggravate the rest 'of them'. Others might think we are getting high and mighty and will need to bring us down a peg or two.

> This reminds me of the story of the American tourist who visits a restaurant in a small Irish town.
>
> On entering the restaurant, he sees a lobster tank with many lobsters. The strange thing is the tank has no lid. He is mystified by this, as he cannot understand why the lobsters don't just crawl up the side and out of the tank. He asks the waiter why the tank has no lid yet the lobsters don't all escape.
>
> The waiter explains that they are local lobsters and as soon as one crawls to the top and is about to escape, the rest of them pull him back down into the tank again.

Yes, there is a danger that as you are about to achieve happiness and success, you get pulled back. If faced with the option of either standing out or fitting in, the only decision really is whether to go for it and run the risk of getting dragged down, or stay where you are in life. Choosing to either fit in or stand out can be a really tough decision either way.

When faced with difficulties or problems, self-leaders ask themselves intuitively: "What gift does this difficulty or problem hide?" They note the answer, which may be something like a new way of thinking, a new way of doing something or the opportunity to take a risk. They understand that determination and stamina are required, when faced with difficulties or problems that have been caused either by their own making or because of some bad luck.

When setting out their desired future, self-leaders do not go out of their way to make life any harder than it has to be. They look for the path of least resistance. However, this does not stop them from taking difficult decisions and staying determined to see them through in the pursuit of the life they want to live. If your instinct is to try and avoid dealing with a difficulty or problem, then the next time you are confronted with such a situation, do your utmost to maintain your energy and commitment to stay determined to step up to the challenge and overcome the difficulty or problem you face.

With this, you might just find yourself tackling difficulties as they arise with more drive and enthusiasm.

Turn to face your fears

We all have fears, many of which we are unaware of. The first step is to become aware and accept that these fears can be rational or irrational. Regardless of whether they are rational or irrational, they are always personal to us as individuals.

Remember, all 'fear' really stands for is:

False Expectations Appearing Real

If you want to lessen your fears, once you are aware of them, you will have to face them. There really is no simple solution. Moving beyond a fear requires you to bring reason to the situation, along with courage and determination. If confrontation is something you fear, then the more you have to deal with it, and stay determined to do so, the less fear it will hold. If you accept the situations in which you find yourself and work at converting them into something positive – which is not easily done – this can have really positive results in your life and work.

> ### EXERCISE
>
> So what are you afraid of? Not having enough money or even too much, being in the right job, being in a relationship, having bad health, a family member dying, achieving your dreams, not being good enough or maybe being too good.
>
> As best you can, name what it is you are afraid of.

Fears are often caused by our thoughts, so we really need to apply our best thinking to them. We need to have a strategy in place setting out what action we can take to deal with these fears. One such strategy is to take each of your worst-case scenarios and face the fear you have about them. Having named your fears, now write them down or say them aloud, for example: "I'm afraid of …". Next, write or say aloud against each one the worst thing that could happen.

Ask yourself if this is really likely to happen or if it is just your mind running wild with your fears. Then write out or say aloud against each of your fears the best thing that could happen.

Doing this will help you to put them in perspective.

Do you play it safe or do you take risks?

If you want to get on in life, you will need to take risks and try out new things. If you keep doing this, it will become a habit, a good habit. This is not easy. If it were, so many more people would be doing it. The ability to take risks in life is a very potent success skill. Most people have never developed this skill. They never move beyond their comfort zones or outside of what they know in their life and work. It is a bit of a cliché, but it really is true that the further you go out on a limb, the easier it is for you to fall. Then again, all the really good fruit is out there on a limb. However, this does not mean having to take big risks. In fact, it is very important not to take big risks.

By their very nature, risks call for caution. You need to look at all your options, choose the one that you believe works best for you, make the decision to go for it and then take the risk.

It takes vision, commitment, dedication and a willingness to take calculated risks. So when embarking on a new challenge or taking a risk, self-leaders make sure they are calculated. As the Roman philosopher, Seneca, said: "It is not because things are difficult that we do not dare; it is because we do not dare that they are difficult." It is about taking small actions and being determined to see them through. It is about taking on even smaller challenges and being determined to deal with and overcome them in pursuit of having a more successful and happier life; to stay determined to face and overcome the difficulties and problems that are thrown up in front of you. As you do this, you will move on in life.

Risk-taking is all about taking small risks, step by step.

Take one risk and, if it works, enjoy the satisfaction that comes with that. Then, and only then, you are ready to move onto the next one, and so on and so forth. When a risk does not pay off, it is important not to beat yourself up. Put it down to experience, learn what you can from it and move back into your comfort zone. Take some time out and build yourself up for the next one, knowing that having already taken a risk, you have expanded your comfort zone. So you will never return to the same place, because you will have made progress in bringing your life further towards where you want it to be.

While some consistency may be reassuring, especially in times of great difficulty, too much of it can begin to seem like inflexibility, or a lack of creativity. As you come to rely on consistency, there is a danger that you will view anything else as a threat. If this happens, it is important to take a step back and the time to look at how living a life of consistency benefits you and what needs to be changed.

Then, go on and make the necessary changes to bring your life forward.

Many people run to safety because of uncertainty in the world. If only people had the courage and determination to run from safety and take risks. There really is a danger right now that what is rigid, secure and inflexible will die; that which adapts and evolves has a greater chance of enduring. The word 'secure' comes from two Latin words: se meaning 'without' and cure meaning 'care' – being free from anxiety and not burdened by excess cares.

How do you view failure?

Trying and failing is better than not trying at all because trying puts you in the game and not just on the sidelines. Being in the game gives you the right to try again. Self-leaders understand the need to garner useful lessons and knowledge from what doesn't work. When something doesn't work, they are prepared to demonstrate remarkable resilience and determination. They develop the ability to bounce back from adversity and failure.

When you try something for the first time and it doesn't work, this doesn't mean you have failed. It just means it didn't work out the way you expected. It took Thomas Edison many attempts before he got the result he wanted with the light bulb.

So you learn. You try. You make 'mistakes'. Just because you failed might not mean you made a mistake. Maybe it was the best you could do at that time and in that situation. The real mistake is to stop trying.

Very often, your head and heart will agree. When that happens, you can be confident in your conclusions. But sometimes the head will say one thing and the heart another.

When this happens, you need to be cautious, extremely cautious. Take a step back and gather some more information and then see where your head is at, along with your heart.

Try to bring a sense of objectivity to it – as much as you can, anyway. Try not to jump right in there and go with the first thing that comes to mind. Look at all the options from all angles. More often than not, an immediate and final judgement is not necessary to deal with the risks people face today, so when your head and heart can't agree, you should hold off. Gather more information. Think some more.

If there is still a conflict between the two, then you need to decide to go with either your head or your heart. Some choose to let the rational head win and thus believe they will have the chance to fight another day. Others go with the heart for no other reason than they feel it is the right thing to do. If it feels right, that is often what works best for them.

> When you have been faced with a major decision and your head and your heart couldn't agree, which one did you go with: the head or the heart? How did it work out for you? Personally, when my head and heart don't match up, I swallow hard and go with my head. Head before heart is not easy but for the fears it has eased, it has worked best for me so far.

Is your glass half full or half empty? One of the most important traits needed to live a life of self-leadership is optimism because it allows you to evolve ideas, stay determined to improve your situation, and hope for a better and more prosperous future for yourself, your family and your colleagues.

Optimism is the one quality most frequently linked to success and happiness. The success and happiness I am referring to here are defined in terms of personal and professional fulfilment and not by wealth, power or social recognition. If these are also part of your definition of success, that is perfectly fine, but they don't have to be.

Pessimists expect bad things to happen. The difference between them and optimists is solely one of expectation, a confidence in the future, but it is a crucial difference which to a large extent determines how people's lives unfold.

Success is

NOWHERE

The pessimist sees 'Success is no where'.

While the optimist sees 'Success is now here'.

Self-leaders focus their thoughts on past successes and triumphs, as opposed to failures and disappointments. When this happens, they feel much more optimistic, determined, confident, constructive and motivated to push on with life. You really will be at your best, most determined, effective and formidable when you focus on the successes you have achieved in your life so far.

Being optimistic does not mean living without difficulties or problems, but knowing you have the ability to come back from setbacks even stronger than before. As long as you have hope and optimism, you will always have the chance of bringing some level of success and happiness into your life and work. Unlike optimists, however, pessimists just will not allow themselves to take on and deal with the opportunities life presents them with. They won't give themselves a chance of bringing real and true success and happiness into their lives and work. They just have that inner belief that "things are not going to work out for me, so why bother doing them in the first place". Equally so, when things are going well, they have to sabotage them – to make them go wrong just to prove they were right in their thinking that "things do not work out well for me".

If at times you find yourself in a pessimistic mood, or if you are just pessimistic by nature, how can you become more optimistic? The method is really quite simple: you need to take an attitude of determination and look for benefits (of any type, big or small) in the situation or circumstances you find yourself, regardless of how bad things are. When you do this and keep persisting in doing it, you will start to experience the same results as optimists. If you maintain this persistence and determination in looking for the benefits, even if you experience failure, you too will start to feel optimistic.

> Philip worked in an organisation where I was doing some consultancy work and asked if he could meet me off site as things were not going too well for him. This came as a surprise to me as he seemed to be completely on top of his job and appeared to be enjoying it.
>
> We met and he really opened up. As he did, the pessimism was plain to see. All the negativity about the state of the economy in the media and in general

conversation was taking its toll on him. He was worried about his job and not having enough money to live on and pay his bills. He had started to lose sleep over it.

While there are very few certainties in life, in his case there were two:

Firstly, he had one of the safest jobs in the organisation. It was a public sector job. With his length of service and specialist skills, other people would lose their jobs before him. So far, not one person had lost their job nor had there been talk of anyone losing their job.

Secondly, with regard to not having enough money, he was not a big drinker, didn't smoke and lived a very simple life. He owned his house and car so there were no big loans to be paid off. Not having money was never going to be a big issue for him.

He had got sucked into all the negativity and pessimism around him.

We agreed that he would focus on being grateful for what he had and would constantly remind himself to have a good day – every day.

When we next met, he explained that a funny thing had happened: when he focused on having a good day (being mindful of all that was good in his life), he just seemed to have a good day and, similarly, when his guard was down and he thought it was going to be a bad day (being pessimistic about all that could go wrong), he was right – he had a bad day even if nothing really went wrong for him.

Try this yourself. At the end of each day, write down three things (more if you like) that you are grateful for.

It could be:

- The car went well
- Lunch was great
- I had a great laugh with one of my colleagues

As the days go by, look to see if you notice even more things to be grateful for in your life.

Self-leaders do their best to live life with gratitude. They work at doing their best to recognise all that is good within their life and work right now. They practise the art of being grateful for everything they have, regardless of how good or bad things are. They believe that, regardless of how things turn out, they will make the best of it anyway. They will, in some way, look at the good in it, learn the lesson and, at some point in the future, turn it to their advantage.

Among other things, they are grateful for good health, a supportive partner, a rewarding profession, healthy children, conscientious employees, prosperity, religious faith, loyal friends and even winning sports teams. The list may be different for each of us, but self-leaders have one thing in common: they realise that if they fall down today, they know they have tomorrow. If they fall down tomorrow, they still have the day after tomorrow. They keep at it. They know they will either succeed or end up being the toughest opponent most of us will ever meet.

Ever the Optimist

> **Exercise**
>
> Who is the most optimistic person you know? What is it about them that would make you say they are optimistic? What person do you meet and feel so much better for having got to spend time with them?

By being optimistic, you dramatically increase your chances of recovering from whatever challenges and problems life throws at you. Leading psychologists from around the world have discovered that, whatever you choose to do with your life, an optimistic outlook will greatly improve your chances of success.

One of the major benefits of being optimistic is that it will help you to move away from seeing things so much in black and white when you view life. When you have an optimistic outlook on life, when challenges come along, you will see your life as a chain of tests rather than a series of successes or failures. Regardless of how things turn out for you, you will learn something from every situation. You will not view it as failing or succeeding but as an opportunity to grow and develop as a person. We know life won't always work out the way we want, and events and situations won't always go in our favour. So be it, that's life. The optimist is determined to keep going, unconcerned by what others might see as failure.

Optimists don't beat themselves up when things don't go right. They have the ability to see what went wrong and what they now need to do to make it right. They can make the changes and move forward in the belief that it will all work out quite successfully. Consequently, they are always open to making the most of how things are or will turn out. This allows for much more success and happiness in their lives, as they are always working towards a positive outcome.

Optimists don't just believe good things will happen, they stay determined to work at making good things happen. They know that, if they want to have success and happiness, they have to make things happen. Looking to where success and happiness may be found, in effect, they search out success and happiness.

WHERE YOU ARE NOW

Regardless of how things are, self-leaders never give in.

If they have to, they change their methods and approaches as to how they handle things as they arise. They give it their all to make their life one of success and happiness. If they don't have success or happiness in their life now, they stay eager and determined to grow, develop and cultivate the life they truly desire and wish for. No matter how small, they keep taking steps to lead them in that direction – to the future they want.

> EXERCISE
>
> What would you do if you knew you could not fail? Consider what two or three things you can do every week, which, if done really well, would change your life.
>
> Then ask yourself: "Why am I not doing them?" When faced with difficulties and problems, why not ask: "How would the self-leader I admire handle this?" Perhaps the best question to ask when it comes to challenging yourself to rise to higher levels of achievement is: "What would the child I once was think of the adult that I have become?"

Ask the above questions as you set out to live your life as a self-leader and remember the Chinese proverb that says: "Without toil, trouble, difficulty and struggle there is no sense of achievement." Don't be afraid of the answers. Just ask the questions and the life you want to live might just answer them.

Congratulations! You have now taken the first step on the path of the self-leadership journey. As you progress along the path, remember to:

- Stay determined

- Be optimistic

- Face your fears

TRAIT 2
GETTING CREATIVE

If a man will begin with certainties,
he shall end in doubts; but if he will
be content to begin with doubts, he
shall end in certainties.

Francis Bacon

In the bogs of East Galway there was once a contest between two turf cutters. Whoever could cut the most turf in twelve hours would be the winner. With shiny, sharpened sleáns (the tool used to cut turf), the two contestants approached their designated bog areas.

From the moment the contest began, one turf cutter cut continuously. For the entire twelve hours, he never once stopped cutting turf. The other contestant cut for an hour and then stopped to rest for ten minutes. And then, like clockwork, he continued to do this for the rest of the day. At the end of the twelve hours, the number of pieces of turf that had been cut was counted to see who had cut the most. It was the man who rested every hour who won the contest by a dramatic margin.

Amazed and confused, his fellow contestant inquired about the winner's secret. Without hesitation, the winner freely told him: "Every time I stopped to rest, I sharpened my sleán." This meant it stayed sharp and cut the turf quicker and easier, unlike the other man's sleán, which got blunter and blunter as the day wore on.

This is true for ourselves, too. We all need to stop regularly to take time to sharpen our mind and rest our body if we want to be truly creative in our life and work. Getting creative will empower you to move in an upward spiral of growth, change and continuous improvement. It is important to identify what works best in helping you to rest and relax, thus renewing yourself and enabling you to be creative and have the stamina to achieve the life you want to live.

A good place to start is to allocate some quality time to thinking about the life you are living and the life you want to be living and then thinking creatively about how you can bridge the gap. This is all about knowing where it is you want to bring your life and getting creative about how best to get there. It means having the courage to take time out to build up your energy and let your creative juices flow in the pursuit of the life you want to be living. One of the best ways to do this is to know what activities give you energy and what activities take your energy. Then you can see what to spend more of your time on in order to build up your energy and creativity.

One activity that gives me energy and fuels my creativity is reading and this is something I try to do on a daily basis. I feel fully justified in paying the price of a book and investing the time in reading it, if only to get one new idea or a different insight into myself, those around me or life in general. I attend a lot of meetings. Sometimes they end early, and at other times I arrive early for the next meeting, so I frequently have time to spare between meetings. I always like to have a book or magazine in the car and this has often proved to be the best reading time for me. Of course, not everyone is interested in or has the time to read so, if this is the case for you, perhaps try talking CDs in your car. They can be great company, particularly on long journeys. The library is a great source to access books and CDs without having to break the bank.

Often our most creative thoughts, or a truth that we learn about ourselves or life, come in the quietest of moments. I had the opportunity to go on a sailing holiday with a friend fourteen years ago. She wanted to learn to sail, whereas I had no great desire to do so. Yet, as the holiday went on, the sailing became more and more enjoyable. Towards the end of the week, I just had one of those moments when I realised this was something I wanted to pursue: this was the perfect holiday and sailing was the hobby for me. Fourteen years on, I am still sailing and it just gets better and better. My friend also had one of those moments during the week: she discovered that sailing was just not for her. Self-leaders try different things as they know it is only by trial and error that they learn what gives them more energy and makes them more creative.

The energy exercise is a great tool to help you identify the activities that not only drain your energy but more importantly give you energy to be creative and stay the course in pursuit of the life you want to be living, both personally and professionally. Complete the following exercise – and then work at incorporating the activities from Column 2 into your daily life. Those who are more rested, relaxed, focused and continually allow themselves to be renewed and creative will perform better than those who are not.

EXERCISE

List all the activities that drain energy from you and then list all of the activities that give you energy.

1. What drains my energy	2. What gives me energy
Examples:	Examples:
Cooking	Listening to music
Shopping	Sailing
Driving	Going to the cinema
Cleaning the house	Reading
Gardening	Good company
	Travelling
	Writing
	Meditating

In times of stress, fatigue and tiredness, you will discover that most of your time and energy is spent doing activities that drain your energy (Column 1), rather than doing those that give you energy (Column 2).

When you find yourself in this situation, you need to shift from doing what is in Column 1 to doing more of what is in Column 2.

Now, remember what takes my energy (such as cooking) might give you energy; and what gives me energy (for instance, travelling) might just drain your energy, so this exercise is unique to each of us.

There is a real need to be relaxed and rested if you are to be at your best and allow yourself to become creative.

When you engage in activities that let you relax as well as give you energy, you are taking the first step in nurturing your creativity, thus allowing new ideas and thoughts to bubble up from within you. Doing the activities you listed in Column 2 will enable you to start believing you are a creative person with the capacity to take a creative approach to your life and your work.

How Creative Do You Think You Are?

> **Exercise**
>
> When you hear the word creativity, what comes to mind?
>
> Do you see yourself as being a creative person? If so, why, and if not, why not?
>
> What has been the most creative thing you have done lately – have you looked at setting up a business, learned to dance, listened to music, read a poem, joined a writers' group, or overcome a serious problem with some lateral thinking?

Only a minority of people believe they are creative. Most people are not educated to value and encourage creativity.

Creative confidence is not about being certain of the answers, but about being certain that you will find the answers yourself.

You will, indeed, face challenges along the way. If you allow yourself to be creative, you need have no fear, for the answers will come to point you in the right direction.

Who comes to mind when you think of people who are creative? Most people find the really creative ones a little left of centre. But I don't mean creativity to that extent, just letting a little more creativity into your life and work. Be a little more creative in the decisions you make and how you deal with challenges that arise as you pursue the life you want to live.

You have to be creative in how you respond to the challenges of life if you are to live a life of self-leadership. Self-leaders accept the challenge of allowing creativity to flourish yet, at the same time, ground this creativity in a way that it can best serve how they want to live their life.

As Einstein said: "Imagination is more important than knowledge. For knowledge is limited to all we now know and understand, while imagination embraces the entire world, and all there ever will be to know and understand." Nothing exists that was not once an idea, which the English poet William Blake echoed when he wrote: "Everything starts in the imagination." So many things in the natural and human world start as a seed; ideas and visions are seeds of potentially great things. Self-leaders use creativity to challenge the status quo of where they are in life and where they want to be in the future. They do this in a practical and realistic manner.

You cannot get creative just by reading about it or watching it: there is a need to throw yourself into it. Creativity is not limited by circumstances. You have to get stuck in there and get your hands dirty to allow it to have a real and genuine impact on your life; to allow creativity to inform you where you want your life and work to go.

It should be remembered that the essence of creativity is limitless. Over and over again, people drop creative ideas because they do not come to immediate fruition, not realising that if they had stayed focused on the life they want to live, it would have eventually become real. In Ancient Greek, there are two words for time: 'chronos' meaning linear or chronological time, and 'kairos' meaning at the right time, a passing moment that must be grabbed in order for success to be achieved.

You need to keep going, knowing that when the time is right things will fall into place for you. Again, this takes great courage and determination, especially when everything seems against you or even when everything really is against you. But you can, indeed, become a creative thinker. Keep working at this, particularly at times when you do not seem to be able to create great ideas.

To launch yourself anew, get out of your head.

You need to act. That is often what you are doing when you get creative – getting out of your head, yet in a structured way.

This allows you to move forward with your life.

Invest in your creativity

When was the last time you were really rested and relaxed? Was it at the end of a holiday or maybe when you had something cancelled at the last moment and had some unexpected time for yourself. How did you feel – more confident, less stressed, clear-headed, even creative and more energised? You will need to feel all these things if you are going to set out the life you want to live, and then have the courage and determination to make the changes needed to see it happen.

Exercise

Take some time to answer the following questions:

What stops you from taking time out to rest, relax and get creative?

Is it that you would feel guilty because you have so much to do that wouldn't be getting done?

Or do you not feel worthy of taking time out for yourself as you have to keep going to meet the demands being placed on you by everyone around you?

Could it be that if you took some time out, you might just really get to see how your life is and that's not a nice thought for you?

So go on and answer the question – what is really stopping you from taking time out to rest, relax and get creative? We can't change something unless we know what it is. You need to first identify it. Living these traits can then help you overcome what is holding you back.

What would help you now to take some quality time out, creating the space to reflect on and set in motion ways of becoming a self-leader in your own life and working towards the life you want to live? Perhaps getting up a few minutes earlier in the morning or switching off the television a little earlier in the evening to create some quiet time for the questions and exercises in this book? Would buying a writing pad or a Dictaphone to record your thoughts and ideas help? If so, just go and do it.

We all have our own strategies for how best to do this – see what works best for you.

Once you have identified the best strategy for you – go for it! Is it that you don't know how to take time out to rest, relax and get creative? If this is the case for you, go back and review your answer to the question: "What gives you energy?" Doing something from that list is a great start. It might take a lot of trial and error to discover what does work for you when it comes to resting, relaxing and getting creative.

> One night, I got to hear a speaker talk about his need to start every day with a fifteen minute meditation. This calmed him down and got him grounded so as to be better positioned to deal with and take on the challenges of the day in a more creative and energised way. (His weakness was that he allowed himself to be pulled in different directions during the course of his working day.) At the end of the talk, he was asked what he does on really long and busy days. His answer: on days like that, he usually does thirty minutes of meditation!

Taking time out will allow you to keep on learning how to live and make the most of the life you are living.

Self-leaders allow themselves the time to be silent, and so they begin to cultivate the power of the imagination, which helps them move towards what they want their life and work to be about. For you, this time out may only be ten to fifteen minutes once a week. This is a great start and will give you something solid to build on. Make the most of this time and use it constructively. It is not about looking back over the past and digging up regrets and mistakes or just day-dreaming about the future. Look at where you want to go and what you are doing about it.

Work at developing a mechanism that allows you to take time out on a regular basis. Space and time will let you gather your energy and thoughts and stop yourself being pulled in different directions on a daily basis. Once you have discovered what works for you to achieve this, have the courage and determination to just do it on a daily basis. Any time spent allowing yourself to recharge your batteries and get creative is not wasted, even if it is just taking a few minutes out to be quiet, to just stand back from all the hustle and bustle around you. This alone will improve your understanding of what is going on for you at any given time and how best you can respond to it. You need to be aware of what it is you are reacting to at any given time and work out how you can positively respond to it instead. (If you are reacting to what is going on around, you are not in charge – only by responding do you get to take control of the situation.) You need to not only look at what is happening but also why it is happening in the first place. It will also give you the opportunity to become aware of the different choices you may have and to think about the implications of each option. This, in turn, will improve your decision-making abilities. If you can ensure you have regular times out, it will also allow you to learn from living.

Self-leaders know that the more they are able to maintain their energy and sense of creativity, the more resilient they will be, the more they will be able to keep going and the more likely they will be to go on and live the life they want to live.

They understand that taking time out to build up their energy and creativity will allow them to move forward in the face of their fears and doubts.

In order to live your life the way you want to, there is a need to invest time and money in making yourself a self-leader in your field. For many people, undertaking personal and professional development is an expensive business but it is also a great investment.

By constantly investing in yourself, attending training seminars and exposing yourself to the latest relevant books and information, you can sharpen skills and develop talents that will help you to be both creative and practical in approaching how best to bring your life forward. The growth of your life and work is directly comparable with that of your own self-growth and the level to which you are prepared to get creative to see this happen.

Taking time out to reflect on how you are living will allow you to be so much better positioned to make those all-important course corrections every week, and so continually move towards living the life you want. This time out will allow you to look at mistakes that may have occurred, to learn from them and make sure they are not repeated.

Harnessing your creativity

Getting creative is one thing, but if this doesn't lead you forward in life, then it is like knowledge without action. What is the point of having all the knowledge yet not turning it into action? Ultimately, it really will be about action and not knowledge alone. And what is the point of getting creative if it doesn't bring you forward in your life and work? It is not enough to just get creative if there is no tangible outcome leading you to where it is you want to be in your life.

Getting creative means taking action and this, in turn, means having to make changes in your life. It requires moving from the known to the unknown – and most people find it difficult dealing with or making changes within their own lives and work.

Self-leaders understand that they have to deal with and make changes in pursuit of the life they want to live.

> When you hear the word 'change', what comes to mind for you? Do you see change as something frightening or do you see it as a challenge to be dealt with, or even an opportunity to grow and develop in your life and work?
>
> When it comes to dealing with or making changes within my own life and work, the following quote from W.B. Yeats comes to mind:
>
> "All changed, changed utterly."

> This has been true for so many of the major changes in my life, including going to live as a monk and then, eight years later, dealing with the upheaval of leaving the monks.
>
> On a professional level, it also applied when I left my secure, pensionable job to be self-employed.

Yes, change can be dangerous and challenging because it involves moving from the known to the unknown. Regardless of how you have dealt with change in the past, it really is up to you to make sure all change starts with you. When you do this, you have control over what you want to change and how this can best be done.

If making a change is a major issue for you, then try taking small actions. There really is nothing wrong with moving forward slowly. Taking small actions can still take you forward.

Never be afraid of celebrating small actions within life and work. The Chinese philosopher Lao Tsu believed: "You will achieve the great task(s) by a series of small actions." To learn and change also involves repetition, so be willing to be incredibly patient. It is also crucial to focus on the success of small beginnings. Most success starts small. Even the Irish airline Ryanair started with only one plane back in 1985. It has gone on and grown to become the most profitable airline in Europe. From the outset, they have done this by being very creative and following through on what they know works best for them as a business in small, incremental ways.

This is your life and it is worth investing time and energy into getting creative to see how best to make changes to improve it. Self-leaders take time to identify the changes that have the potential of moving them forward in pursuit of the life they want to be living. Having identified them, they get creative and search out ways to implement them.

When dealing with and making changes in their life, self-leaders remain mindful of the following obstacles that can arise:

Firstly, at times, they can get confused and have no clear direction, other than they know that they want to bring their life to a better place. A possible solution to this is to accept and then deal with the fact that they may have an investment in being confused.

Clarity means decisions, change and a commitment to move forward in life.

They understand that one way through this is to be inspired to change and see the possible benefits for their future. Another is to make it more painful not to change, staying trapped where they are with things going from bad to worse, so that they have no choice but to change, and this spurs them on.

Secondly, they might feel they have too much invested in their current situation. They might, in effect, say: "This would be so painful to change." Then they tend to focus on the worst that could happen and not on the best that could happen.

If this is the case, they accept that being open to change is not always easy and, more often than not, it is very difficult. For the most part, it involves overcoming difficulties, problems and challenges in your life and work. Remember, if you associate change with pain and loss, why would you ever want to change? Often it is not the change that is painful, but people's resistance to this change, their attachment to old ways, beliefs and concepts that causes their pain. It is due to them wanting to hold onto the past rather than let go and move on with their life.

Where You Are Now

We all know the demands being placed on each and every one of us today. It is constant; we are always accessible through mobile phones, email and so on. It is never-ending; the world wants our attention right now. Yes, even if this means dropping what we are doing. People want results instantly, no time to wait (or waste) but the challenge is to not always get sucked into what the world wants and demands of you all of the time. Work at building up the courage to take time out for you – to allow yourself the time and space to see how best to allow creativity into your life and work. Allowing this creativity shows you the best way forward for your life and work.

If you are to move forward with life, in the direction you truly want to move in, this will demand that you be creative in how you deal with and overcome the many difficulties, problems and challenges that may be faced along the way.

By taking time to think and allow creativity to flourish, you will be able to see the options available and then make decisions. This means you will be able to make the right decisions, giving clarity to where you want your life to go. This clarity will often engender confidence, persistence, resilience and creativity in you. Taking time out will also allow you to remind yourself of what is important to you, both personally and professionally. It will give you the chance, at times, to disengage and not get drawn into everything that is happening around you.

Most people live busy and full-on lives. So look forward and anticipate any possible quiet times that may be coming your way.

Then box this time off for a little creative thinking, an opportunity to reflect on your own. This time out should allow you to process all that has happened or is happening within or around you at any given time. It gives you the chance to see through the confusion and what you need to do to move forward in pursuit of the life you want, in a creative yet realistic manner.

Congratulations! You have now taken the second step on the path of self-leadership. As you progress along the path, remember to:

- Take time out

- Do the things that allow you to rest, relax and get creative

- Allow creativity to show you the way forward in your life and work

Trait 3
Playing to your Strengths

We are not creatures of circumstance; we are creators of circumstance.

Benjamin Disraeli

My good friend David, is a great example of someone who chose to play to his strengths and reap the rewards for having done so. He had been asked to join a new start-up advertising agency, leaving behind a secure job with the government, in which he had been very successful.

He did not know much about advertising – but the founder did. What David had been asked to bring to this new company was his expertise in financial controls, money management, people management, honesty and organisational skills. For the most part, these were the very same strengths he was not able to use in his current job.

A decision had to be made. He could either play it safe and let his present job grind him down or play to his strengths and take on the risk and challenge of going to work for a new start-up company.

The decision was easy for him. Life was too short, his job was getting to him, and the new opportunity was both too good to turn down and too much of a challenge to turn away from.

One of David's key strengths is money management.

He oversees and manages the money coming in to and going out of the company. He has built up and honed this strength so successfully that, fifteen years later, the new start-up has become an international player on the advertising scene with over fifty employees.

Find your flaws and fix them! So many people have been advised to do this. It will keep you challenged, nicely rounded and humble – and it will keep your boss happy! This only tells you what to do with your unique complement of strengths and weaknesses: maintain the former and fix the latter. But, in fact, what people really need to do is play to their strengths and make their weaknesses irrelevant. This really is by far the most effective strategy in living a life of success and happiness. It is so important to discover what you don't like doing and then stop doing it.

Most people have been brought up in the belief that they will grow and develop most by working on their weaknesses.

This is simply not true. You will not grow and develop the most as a human being by focusing on your areas of weakness.

The truth is you will learn, grow and develop the least in your areas of weakness. Any learning, growth and development attained will be hard won. This does not change over time – it applies equally regardless of age. It is as true for a ten year old as for a sixty year old. The fact is you would be far better off investing all your drive, time and focus on your strengths.

WHAT IS MEANT BY A 'PERSONAL STRENGTH'?

The definition of 'a strength' is an activity that makes you feel strong.

Strengths can be found in activities in which you exhibit consistent, near-perfect performance. They are those specific activities at which you do well and for which you still retain a powerful appetite. It feels easy. It feels like you don't need to try very hard. It feels like an activity that, for some reason, proved quite simple for you to pick up. You learned it quickly. It is something innate that comes from within; something that you find easy to tie into, to use, to grow and to develop. When you are using your strengths, you don't struggle to concentrate.

Instead, you naturally stay focused and time speeds up, and you still feel focused and time speeds up some more.

Skills are something we learn, such as computer skills, while a strength is having a really keen interest and a natural ability to hone and develop such a skill. Having a strength in a particular area will allow you to pick up and use these skills so much more easily than those who don't have a strength there. Not having a strength in this area won't stop you from learning new skills but they will be much harder to learn than for someone who has a natural strength there.

Strengths can be found in activities that draw you back to them time and again, the activities you can't help volunteering for. These are where your strengths lie. They are the ones that keep your interest and your concentration with almost no effort; the activities that leave you feeling strong, fulfilled and powerful.

Strengths are not only activities for which you have some natural talent; they are also activities that strengthen you.

When using them, you feel powerful, authentic and confident and challenged in the best sense of the word. As such, they are self-reinforcing. Left to their own devices, they will – and must – be expressed.

The most successful people sculpt their life and jobs so they spend a disproportionate amount of time doing what they love. This is no accident. It happens because they stay alert to those activities they don't like and cut them out as quickly as possible. They do their best to guard the time they can spend doing what they love.

People really do grow and develop most in the areas of their greatest strength. Now, being strong at something is more than just being good at it. Being strong at something means this is an area you want to pursue. Often, for reasons unbeknown to you, it is an area in which you want to grow, develop and learn. It is as if you have a calling to it and just love to do it, regardless of the feedback you get – which is often good and gets better as you grow and develop this strength. You feel pulled towards this activity, even with the many doubts and fears you may have about doing it.

Being True to Yourself

If there is one thing that self-leaders do consistently, it is integrity to do what matters most to them.

When you pay close attention to what you say and do – and make sure both these things are focused on long-term aspirations, rather than the emotion of the moment – you discover, miraculously, that you have developed a better attitude. Acknowledge and accept that it takes tremendous commitment, determination, discipline and even courage to continuously engage in this practice of alignment.

When you do, the chances of having success and happiness in life and work are so much greater.

Self-leaders find, when their words and actions are in alignment, they feel as if they are on track – in the zone, so to speak. When this happens, they seem to attract the right people and situations into their lives and work. They don't believe in words but only in behaviours. They stick with what they know to be right. This can often call for great personal courage because sticking with what you know is right, when all the odds are against you, is not easy.

Self-leaders make sure their words match where they are heading. If your words, actions and intentions match, it all works out without fail. Highly accomplished people use language in an instinctive or intuitive way, always focusing on what they are trying to accomplish. They are confident when they commit to progress with a strong narrative and matching deeds. They chip away and eventually overwhelm toxic thoughts and feelings.

PUTTING YOUR STRENGTHS TO WORK

No man or woman will find the best way to do a thing unless he or she loves to do that thing.

Japanese proverb

Strengths, correctly identified, reveal a person's capacity.

Yet, they are no guarantee of success. Even without this guarantee it is still great advice to identify your strengths and tailor your work to these. A person will excel only by amplifying strengths, never by simply fixing weaknesses.

Get your strengths together and make your weaknesses irrelevant. Your strengths are your greatest asset. Each and every person is at their most creative and shows their best judgement precisely in their areas of greatest strength.

It is also known that, while you continue to learn throughout adulthood, you will learn the most in those areas where you already know most, where your synaptic branches are already thick and strong. On the emotional side of things, you know you will be more resilient, persistent, self-confident and effective in areas where you have developed some mastery.

You will only be able to transfer these powerful feelings to new challenges if these new challenges are substantially similar to your existing areas of mastery.

Exercise

One of my strengths is to stand in front of people and give presentations and facilitate meetings. When I'm doing this:

- People tell me that it just seems to come so naturally, like I'm not trying at all
- That I really seem to be enjoying it
- That I really hold people's attention

It is an activity that people are always volunteering me for.

Giving presentations and facilitating meetings are two things that I have improved in and this has contributed to my further personal and professional development.

They come easily and I love the opportunity to do them. I search out and look for opportunities to do them.

At times (very many times), I'm nervous about how they'll go. Will the topic be right? Will I have too much or too little material? What happens if I lose track or the audience don't like what I'm saying? These are all real and honest fears and doubts, yet they are not enough to stop me from getting up there and speaking.

What activity (or activities) do people say just seems to come so naturally to you – it's like you're not trying when you do it?

> That you really seem to enjoy doing it?
>
> That it holds your attention or that of others if they are involved?
>
> The activity that people are always volunteering you for?
>
> Having answered the above, what would you honestly say are your strengths? If you are struggling with this exercise, think of the leaders you chose, for it may be the very things they are strong at that you are strong at, too.
>
> Over the coming days and weeks, when doing certain activities, look to see if they meet the above criteria. When you identify one that does, you can be pretty sure you're looking at one of your strengths.

If you want to bring about and/or build on success and happiness, most of your learning should be targeted towards those areas where you have already achieved some level of mastery. If you have a natural ability to solve problems or to build relationships or to compete or to anticipate the needs of others, you will get the most bang from your learning buck from stretching, refining and focusing on these abilities.

Brian is an accountant working for one of the top accountancy firms in Ireland. He came to me even though he was really successful, having been made a partner at a very young age. The problem was, he was not enjoying his job and this was now affecting his life outside work.

He worked with some very high net-worth individuals (financially speaking) but they didn't seem to be enjoying life either. They were making lots of money but that is all they seemed to be doing.

What he was very good at was doing their accounts but he was much stronger in the manner in which he could relate to them.

They paid for his expertise in accountancy but they wanted his time. He wanted to give them more time to look beyond just doing their accounts and to the life they were living as a whole but he was only getting paid to do their accounts. He had really had enough.

I worked with him to identify this strength: he is able to get people to spend time with him, and stop and look at the bigger picture of their life, not just the work they are doing and the money they are making. He gains their trust in such a way that they are prepared to work with him to see beyond the making of money. They identify what else they would like to be doing in their life – what hobby they would like to take up, the interests they would love to pursue, be it in the world of charitable organisations or in the arts and so on. His vision is to now work with individuals to see the bigger picture of

> their life and not just that of their finances and making money.
>
> The challenge at present is to develop a plan of action for him to see this vision become a reality. He is excited about focusing in on and using his strengths and yet, at the same time, he is apprehensive because he knows, no matter what happens, big changes are coming in his life and work right now.

What is meant by a 'personal weakness'?

The most useful definition of a weakness is an activity that makes you feel weak. It's an activity that, no matter how proficient you may (or may not) be at it, consistently produces negative emotional reactions. Your weaknesses have a 'no matter how hard I try, I just can't get excited by the prospect of this' quality to them. No matter how much you try to like them, the outcome will always be the same: negative. And when you are doing the activity, all you can do is look forward to it being finished.

While the activity may need to be done, it gives you no pleasure. It is a struggle to stay engaged or in any way interested in the task at hand. If you have to learn more about the activity because it is a requirement of your job, you will do so, yet you are still not inquisitive about the activity itself.

There is no real desire to get better at it. You don't have any great interest in reading up on it or learning more about it.

Having done the activity, or while doing it, you find you are asking yourself again and again: "Why do I have to put myself through this?" The activity leaves you feeling not only physically tired but also emotionally and intellectually drained.

If time seems to stand still when you are undertaking or endeavouring to work on or achieve something, and it's a real pressure or strain to focus on, then take the hint. What you are trying to complete is something that is a weakness of yours. When undertaking any activity that has these effects, a clear message is being sent that doing this activity is making you use your weaknesses. There may be no good explanation for this but you need to recognise when it is happening and accept that it really is up to you to do something about it.

No matter how often you do it, something that is a weakness will always seems to slow you down and drain your energy. What you need to do is spend less time on your weaknesses and achieve more using your strengths. Stopping activities that weaken you is a real challenge. You will have to develop strategies that will allow you to back off from using your weaknesses. What is really important is that you devote time to learning what weakens you and devise a few of your own ideas on how to manage and overcome them.

Identifying Your Weaknesses

If you are to accurately identify your weaknesses as well as your strengths, you must be similarly clear-headed and strong-willed. No matter what others may tell you, when you confess a certain activity weakens you, this does not mean you disrespect the activity. It simply means this activity consistently produces negative emotional reactions in you.

The most respectful, responsible, lasting and effective thing you can do is to work out a way to cut it out of your life. You never look forward to it and are exhausted afterwards – these are two sure signs of a weakness.

Living a life of self-leadership calls for total honesty with yourself. If you allow honesty to direct the way forward, you will have a much greater chance of living a life of happiness and success.

Confusingly, you may experience some achievement when undertaking these activities – nevertheless they leave you feeling depleted, drained, frustrated or merely bored. To both have and sustain success and happiness in life, there is a need to recognise these weaknesses for what they are and do your utmost to let them go, and then focus your attention on using your strengths. If strengths are activities that strengthen you, then weaknesses are the opposite; they are the activities that weaken you. A sign of a weakness is when you are undertaking an activity that you are good at – other people may even tell you that you are good at it – but as an activity it doesn't work for you. It is not something you look forward to doing, it doesn't hold your interest while doing it and, more often than not, you have no great desire to learn about the activity or how you could become better at doing it.

When it comes to weaknesses, there is a need to first identify them for what they are – weaknesses. While it may not be possible to get rid of them, having identified them, you will be better placed to minimise their impact on the activities and roles you have to undertake. Work at acknowledging them the moment they appear. Work your way through them but make sure you limit the time spent doing them. There is also another big challenge here, in that once you have recognised your weaknesses, you can't complain about them any more, as you now know that it really is up to you to go and do something about them.

Exercise

What would you honestly say are your weaknesses? What activities do you have to do on a regular basis that:

You are just not inquisitive about?

You have no desire to get better at?

You don't want to read up on or learn more about? It's a case of asking yourself again and again: "Why do I have to put myself through this?" These are the activities that leave you feeling not only physically tired but also emotionally and intellectually drained.

Over the coming days and weeks, when doing certain activities, look to see which ones meet the above criteria.

When they do, you can be pretty sure you're looking at one of your weaknesses.

Having identified your weaknesses, the challenge is to stay focused on your strengths and to do your utmost to concentrate as much of your energy and time as possible on developing these.

Try to stop doing the activities that call on your weaknesses, if this is feasible, perhaps by building relationships with others who can help you or, if possible, by paying for the services of others to carry out these activities for you.

> Philip, a social worker, is great at dealing with confrontational situations within his workplace. Any time a situation looks like it is going to blow up into a confrontation, Philip is always called for.
>
> There is no doubt that he will talk people down, get people to back off and is able to bring the whole situation to a fairly calm conclusion.
>
> He's excellent at doing this but it's not one of his strengths – others have identified it as one of his key strengths, but it's not. How do we know?
>
> After every confrontational situation, he feels not only physically tired but also emotionally and intellectually drained. Every time he has dealt with such a situation, he asks himself: "Why do I have to put myself through this?" In relation to dealing with or becoming better at managing confrontational situations, he is not in any way inquisitive, has no desire to get better at it and in no way wants to read up on or learn more about it. He's very good at dealing with confrontational situations yet it is just not one of his strengths.

If you have to take on responsibilities or undertake a role that frequently calls on your weaknesses, a great way to overcome this very successfully is to look for partnerships.

Seek out others who have strengths in areas in which you are weak and vice versa. Then see how you can work with each other, building on your combined strengths and minimising the weaknesses.

If none of this is possible, look to see if you can drop the role or activity, or at least change it in some way. Is there an area in which you could use your strengths? If none of these are possible, there is one last thing you can try: to find one aspect, any aspect, of the role or activity that brings out your strengths and strive to always keep this aspect at the front of your mind. This strategy will involve more mind games than the others, but it might just be the only option available to you. It means saying "Yes" to acknowledging what calls on you to use your weaknesses but "No" to dwelling on them.

More importantly, it allows you to become aware of and acknowledge what you are strong at and to search out and sustain ways in which your strengths can be put to best effect.

Staying alert

As you grow and develop as a self-leader, you must keep your senses alert to those aspects of your role that bore or drain you. Whenever you become aware of some aspect you dislike, do not try to work through it. Instead, cut it out of your life as fast as you can. The longer you put up with aspects of your work you don't like, the less successful and happy you will be.

As quickly as you can, stop doing them, and then see what the best of you, now focused and unfettered, can achieve.

Having a life of success and happiness, regardless of how this is defined, means guarding your time to be able to do what you love to do. Stay attentive to what you spend time on. But this shouldn't stop you from trying out other things, testing new skills and undertaking different tasks. The important thing is to make sure you spend as much time as possible on what brings you the greatest results and to identify the activities that get in the way of this happening. Identify them and then take the appropriate action to stop doing them. The better you do this, the more success and happiness you will have.

This is what the theory and research would have us believe and no doubt it is true. While it may be true, it's just not practical for the vast majority of people. In order for this to happen and the work environment to change to allow this, there needs to be a very big paradigm shift. There is no doubt that workplaces would be radically altered for the better if this paradigm shift were to happen.

If your role represses your strengths, you may be able to hold them in for a short while, but every day the pressure will build and build, until they burst out like a cork from a shaken champagne bottle. Don't let it come to that. If you are heading that way, go back and look at your answer to what gives you energy from the exercise in Trait 2: GETTING CREATIVE. Pick out one of the activities that gives you energy and go and do it.

Keep doing this activity or others from your list until you have a sense that you can now minimise using your weakness and start using one of your strengths. If you wait for the perfect moment, situation or job to utilise your strengths, you may be left waiting. With this in mind, you need to focus on using your strengths at every opportunity. See where you can use them and then do so.

Once you have employed your strengths and achieved some initial success, other people – often well-meaning people, but more often than not, people who are unaware of your strengths – will insist on offering you new opportunities, new assignments and new roles. Some of these may call upon your strengths, but many will not. The secret to sustained success and happiness lies in knowing which activities engage your strengths and which do not. You then need to have the self-discipline and confidence to reject the latter. If you do want to live the life you wish for, you must discover your strengths and cultivate them. What makes sustained success so elusive is that, unfortunately, our strengths are rarely left to their own devices. This is so often the case within the workplace. As you use your strengths and have success, you get noticed. You start to be seen as someone who is doing a great job. Then, because employers want to recognise and support this, they end up promoting you, often into jobs that don't allow you to use the very same strengths that made you a success in the first place.

> Sean came to see me because he had been offered a promotion. The new role was to manage a team of sales people. It was a great opportunity for him.
>
> His excellent work had been recognised and now they wanted him to lead the team and were prepared to pay him handsomely for it. While on one level he wanted to

accept it, on another he knew it just didn't sit right with him.

We worked together on identifying his strengths.

He was a great people person; he could really engage with people and get them motivated. These were both strengths that just came naturally to him – when doing either or both of these, he was very upbeat and energised. He was a great talker and very likeable.

Having worked together to identify his strengths, we then identified his weaknesses. He was no good in situations of confrontation or having to deal with administrative work. When called upon to engage in either or both of these, he would end up very downbeat and worn out.

As it was, his strengths were being used on a daily basis and, if he were to accept the new role as manager, for the most part his weaknesses would be called upon.

At the end of our time together, he decided not to take the new position but offered to stay as a sales person and work on training and developing other members of the team. He was so good at this that he now moves between different teams and sales locations within the company, using both of his strengths and getting very well paid for it.

Yes, there was a big push from his ego (and family) to take the job but, thankfully, he didn't and he's better off for it.

Where You Are Now

While you may discover what you don't like doing, if you didn't already know, it might not be possible to stop doing these things right now. Again, it's a matter of identifying them, accepting you don't like doing them and searching out ways to stop doing them. If this is just not going to happen, look to see if you can minimise your involvement in any way. If not, then it's about trying to minimise the impact on yourself when you are undertaking the activity.

The easiest, fastest and most successful way to achieve the life you want to live is by building on your strengths and minimising or overcoming your weaknesses. Self-leaders do their best to give attention to the things that matter most to them. They become an authority on what is important to them, know their range of strengths and put them to good use.

Congratulations! You have now taken the third step on the path of self-leadership. As you progress along the path, remember to:

- Identify your strengths

- Let go of your weaknesses

- Put your strengths to work

Trait 4
Having a Vision for your Life and Work

To live is the rarest thing in the
world. Most people exist, that is all.

Oscar Wilde

A visitor to the area came across a man fishing on the east coast of Ireland and this is how the conversation went:
Visitor: How's the fishing going today? The man fishing: The fishing is good here every day.

Visitor: You fish every day?

The man fishing: Oh yes, I fish every day and then sell what I've caught to the local restaurants. I make some nice money so I get to eat in a nice restaurant. Having eaten, I then enjoy the rest of the evening before getting up the next day after a nice long sleep to go fishing again.

Visitor: It seems like you have the makings of a very successful business. If you bought a boat, you could catch a lot more fish. Do this for a while and then you could buy another boat to catch even more fish. Keep doing this and next thing you know, you have a fleet of boats and you're catching lots of fish and making lots of money.

The man fishing: What would I do when I have this fleet of boats and am making all this money?

Visitor: Sell it, of course, and then you can retire.

The man fishing: Having retired, what would I do then?

Visitor: Having retired, you could go fishing every day.

The man fishing: Why would I put myself through all that hassle when I can go fishing every day anyway?

Both had a vision: they just had different ways of getting there.

Self-leaders see things differently. They work at becoming aware of all the possibilities the future holds, regardless of the circumstances they may find themselves in or the crippling fear they may be feeling about bringing their life forward.

They define the future they want for their life and work. This definition or image of the future is the vision they want, giving a very vivid picture of where they want their life to be at some point in the future.

When you write it down, this clear picture of the future you want becomes your vision statement – a written statement setting out a description of where you want your life to be in the future. Having this vision statement will allow you to see and be reminded on a constant basis of where it is you want your life and work to be. Having this clear picture of the life you want to live, like the fisherman above or Margaret, who's story follows on the next page, will allow you to see what it is you need to both add and subtract from your life to achieve your vision.

When it comes to success and happiness, people often talk and think in terms of 'having or getting', wanting this or that in their life. At times, it might be about getting things out of their lives or moving away from certain situations. Having a life of success and happiness is not always caused by what you add to your life and work but more often by what you have the discipline to remove from your life and work as you set out your vision.

Margaret came to see me because she felt that life was passing her by, that she was just drifting from day to day.

Life was 'good', her job was going very well and she had a very active social life. Similarly, her partner had a very 'good' job and he also had a very active but, for the most part, a very different social life. They worked very hard, were well compensated for this and got to live very full and active lives. The only thing was, they didn't get to spend a lot of time together.

Margaret wanted to explore other options in her/ their life. She wanted to travel and she wanted to get out of living the hectic city life. Over time, she spoke to her partner and it was agreed that they would need to make serious adjustments to their lifestyle if what she/ they wanted was to happen.

It would mean letting go of:

The big house they have (and the big mortgage repayments) and moving to the countryside

Their high-pressured but very well paid jobs in exchange for something a lot less demanding but, at the same time, a lot lower paid

Their circle of friends and discovering a new group who were now going to share their easy-going and simple lifestyle

The trappings of their current lifestyle, such as the company cars and clothes that go with their jobs.

> Margaret and her partner now have a vision of the life they want to live but they will have to accept that major changes will be needed for this to become a reality.
>
> They must let go of what they have so that other, more meaningful, things can come into their lives.
>
> It will take time for this to happen and they are now in the process of seeing how best they can let go of their current life to make way for a more successful and happier one, which is better suited to them.

HAVING A VISION

Having a vision means setting out what you intend to achieve in life. Most people have one but, for the most part, they have never articulated it or put it down on paper.

> Let me give the following example: Say you want to get from one part of the country to another part 100 miles away on any given day. Well, simply put, that is your vision – to be at a certain destination known to you which is 100 miles away at some point later that day. It is a desired future place that you want to get to.

People are living out a vision for their life every day. If this is not done consciously, then it will be done unconsciously.

What for you would be the benefits of having a vision for your life?

Here are some of the benefits enjoyed by self-leaders:

- A vision gives them something positive to aim for
- A vision brings focus to their efforts
- A vision engenders within them a greater sense of self worth and confidence
- A vision gives meaning and purpose to their life
- A vision gives them something to hope for
- A vision means bringing about positive change within their life and work
- A vision acts as a guide to their decision making

Trait 4 is all about self-leaders having a description of what their life will look like once they have reached their vision and achieved their full potential. The key for them is about making the vision something that touches the heart and soul, something that truly motivates them. They are prepared to give their all in pursuit of this vision. Something that both challenges and stretches them as a person, yet has a real and true chance of being achieved, even if it may take a lifetime, all of their lifetime. You can find your vision by focusing on what is, what you have and what you could be.

Being a self-leader with a vision does not mean you have to set out to save the world. It simply means that you have identified where it is you want to bring your life. Having done this, you then have to go and make it a reality. You need to take ownership and responsibility to see everything you want to achieve in life happen. Self-leaders believe in a better future for themselves and those around them.

YOUR VISION

Developing a vision for your life means creating a picture of the future that is better than the status quo. If your vision does describe a better future and, although challenging, has a realistic chance of being achieved, it will be a great way to motivate you.

Having a vision for your life does not mean having to set out on just one path and one path only and sticking with it.

In fact, the opposite is true. In pursuit of living a life of self-leadership, many things may change along the way, such as your views on success and happiness, your views about yourself as a person, and the circumstances in which you find yourself.

Remember when people are at the end of their lives, it is the relationships they formed and the difference they made in the world that they value most highly. Towards the end of their lives, most people agree that the greatest things they have done, and the legacy they are proudest to leave behind, are what they did to help others.

When you set out on a journey, it is vital to know where you are headed, even if you don't know how you are going to get there. It is important to start with the end in mind, but there is a need to guard against the end being a dead end.

There is a great danger of this happening if you are in such a hurry to set a path for yourself and you do not connect this with what you have set out as your vision.

If you have a vision for your life, you have a direction with focus and clarity. It means having the power of a written structure against which every decision concerning the most effective use of your time, your talents, financial resources and your energies can be effectively measured.

Vision is the ability to see into the infinite future, past the boundaries of your conditioning and present circumstances, to what could be. It means being able to see the life you truly want and how you want to live it, seeing life and what it could be, not just what it has been. It is about being willing to see the present and the future as not just being the same as the past but as something that can be changed for the better.

> Andrew came to see me because he felt his life was going nowhere. He really felt that he was on the treadmill and he was just heading in no particular direction. He had no real energy, enthusiasm or desire for his life as it was and it was as if he was just going through the motions.
>
> Having worked together and agreed where his life was really at and how he wanted to see his life in the future – his vision – we came to the following conclusion:

> That his life needed to be enjoyable and fulfilling, both personally and professionally.
>
> Now, how was this to be done in a practical and realistic manner? You will have to wait until Trait 5: Knowing your Mission to see how we set about seeing his vision become a reality.

DESCRIBING YOUR VISION

When you set out your vision, you need to look at what you want to **eliminate** from your life, what you want to **add** to it and what you want to **leave unchanged**. You need to identify what bothers you. It's then about describing your future vision around these things. Keep what is good, remove what is bad and add what will make the vision one of real success and happiness for you.

True vision is not seen through the eyes of the body but through the eyes of the mind. That is why it is so important to engage your mind when setting out the vision. Regardless of where you are in life, you have the capacity to live a life with vision and imagine a different future. But to have any chance of living out the vision, it needs to excite your mind and touch your heart.

How many people have a clear idea of what living a life of success and happiness means to them? Does it mean having more money, a bigger car, more holidays, a better job and a nice partner? How many people have really taken the time to step back and ask themselves what true success and happiness means to them in their life and work, and what it would be like to live a life of self-leadership in pursuit of their life's vision? If you never define your vision of success and happiness, then nothing is going to change and whatever is most urgent will always get done first. If you only do what is urgent at any given time, your life will not go forward in the way that you would have hoped. Living like this will not give you a successful, happy, fulfilling and productive life. If the most important things are not prioritised and done first, there is a real danger that everything will be treated as equal. Separate the urgent from the important and work on getting the important done.

> Exercise
>
> ○ What does success and happiness mean to you?
>
> ○ What makes you happiest and when are you at your best?
>
> ○ What gives you enjoyment and pleasure and a sense of purpose?
>
> ○ How do you want to grow and develop as a person and what must be done to achieve this?

Asking yourself these questions will lead to the truth of what you are doing with your life and why. If you are brutally honest with yourself, the answers can often be about other people's success and happiness. What it is they have (or very often what you think they have) and your desire to have the same. For a great many people, it has been defined by their parents, the education they have received, their work, their friends or the community in which they were brought up.

What makes your heart pump, but in a good way? What gives you that sense of excitement and adrenalin? When this happens, it can often give a good indication of what success and happiness mean to you.

Yet it is more than this. There is also a need to understand and recognise what you are passionate about and where your potential lies. People who build their lives around their passions using their full potential, generally live far happier and more successful lives.

Only you can define your vision of success and happiness.

What does success and happiness mean to you? Go back and look at your answers to what gives you energy in Trait 2.

When you are doing these activities, do you feel at your most successful and happiest? When you are using your strengths as identified in Trait 3, are you at your most successful and happiest then? Only you know where your own true happiness and success lie.

Defining Your Vision

If you truly want to live a life of success and happiness, there really is a need to define what this means to you. Doing this will provide a focus on what you need to do to achieve this.

This is something that must be done continuously as your definition can and often will change throughout life. What you might have considered to be success and happiness in your twenties might not be the same in your thirties and forties, for example. Even on a daily basis, it is often relative to what you need on that day or at that particular time in your life.

Now, what if you're not in a position to build your life and work around your passions and strengths? Does this mean you can't have success and happiness in your life and work? No, of course not, there is always the future even if it might not be possible to follow your passions and strengths right now.

However, you can still see what you can do right now that will move you in the direction of more success and happiness, either now or in the future.

You can never get to where you want to go unless you know where you are going. The same applies to success and happiness. How do you know what this means to you unless you have taken the time to define it? To begin with, it is enough just to define success and happiness – forget about how you are going to reach it. Right now, that is not important. What is important is stating very clearly what you want and why it is so important to have it. Do this first and then look at how best to achieve it.

In the end, nobody cares how much money they made or what car they drove or what awards they won. You cannot take anything of monetary value with you when you die. It is better not to wait until the end of your life to realise that it was the relationships you had and the actions you took to improve the lives of others that mattered most. Appreciate these things today.

Many people don't even ask themselves what it would mean to be truly successful and happy. For doing so might lead to even greater disappointment. If they set out to discover what they want in their life, knowing this and then believing they can't achieve it might be even more frustrating.

Only you can set out a path that is worth travelling in pursuit of your vision of the life you want. Once you have set out to achieve your vision, you will be successful because you will be on the right path in life. You will not only enjoy the moment of reaching your vision but also the journey there.

Self-leaders set out clearly in their mind where they want their life and work to be in the future. They then put this vision down on paper so it's clearly written in front of their eyes.

Once they have done this, they take the steps needed to make this vision a reality.

Anyone can do incredible things but first they have to have incredible things to do. For the vast majority of people, while the idea of doing incredible things in their life and work sounds appealing, it is just not their reality and is never going to be. At the same time, this shouldn't stop people from having a vision of the life they want; a vision that will stretch them and lead to their personal and professional growth.

EXERCISE

Take some time to answer the following questions and set out a vision of the success and happiness you want for your life and work.

1. Looking at the answers you gave when describing your vision, what do you believe success and happiness mean to you – not in the eyes of your family, friends, neighbours or culture – in the following areas or in any other area(s) you might care to add?

○ Work

○ Relationships

○ Health

○ Financial

○ Spiritual

○ Hobbies and interests

These have not been listed in order of priority as only you can do that. There may be some you want to add and others you want to take out.

2. Why do you believe this means success to you?

3. Having reviewed what success means to you, write a paragraph (keep it to a maximum of four or five succinct sentences) on what this success would look like to you two, three or five years from now – maybe even ten or twenty years from now.

Look at all of the areas of your life that you would like encapsulated in these four or five sentences, e.g. family, work, relationships, friendships, hobbies, interests, health, spiritual, and so on.

Once you have done this, leave it alone for a day.

Then come back to it and see if anything needs to be added or subtracted. Make the necessary changes and, once again, leave it for a day.

When you come back to look at this paragraph once again, see if it states how you want your life to look in the future – this period of time in the future that you identified.

If you need to make any changes, make them, and then leave it alone, once again, for another day.

Having done this, finally take your paragraph of four or five succinct sentences and rework it so that it covers everything you want to say but in one or, at most, two succinct sentences.

This is your vision statement of success and happiness for your life.

After I looked at all the important areas in my life, the following is my own vision statement of success and happiness for my life and work:

My vision is to have the necessary resources to live a healthy lifestyle, doing work that I enjoy, using my strengths and allowing me to travel both personally and professionally.

Has this vision been achieved yet? No, it hasn't but it has been set out and I am prepared to give my all in order to achieve it.

BELIEVE IN YOUR VISION

You have to believe in the vision you have for your life as well as believe that you are worthy of it. If you don't believe you are worthy, then you have to deal with this. You have to look deep inside yourself and ask what is holding you back. Do you really believe you are worthy of success and happiness? Do you really believe in the success and happiness you want, or is it someone else's definition of success and happiness that you are pursuing? If you truly own the vision, there's a much better chance of it becoming a reality. Like all things in life, the more you want it, the more you have to be prepared to do to get it.

Once you have taken ownership of the vision, you will also be much more motivated if you can clearly see how your own willingness to take action can play its part in achieving this vision and seeing it fulfilled. If you truly own your vision, it will have a greater chance of being realised. You may have to develop the belief that you are worthy of the investment in yourself. Once you have worked out what you truly love doing, then you may have to develop the self-belief, faith and courage – if you have not already done so – to go and do what you love doing in pursuit of your vision.

Many people wait for the approval of others before moving forward in pursuit of their vision. Self-leaders very rarely wait for or seek out the approval of others when pursuing a life of success and happiness. They refuse to allow social pressures to dictate how they live their lives, knowing that those who achieve success and happiness live the life they want, often doing so despite social pressures rather than because of them.

Nothing focuses the mind better than a vision you have for your future that moves the heart. Your expectations create the reality. If you believe in the vision, it really can become a self-fulfilling prophecy. Keep doing all you can within your power to make the vision become a reality. Once you take ownership of your vision, it becomes so much better and easier to create this future than to wait for external forces to dictate your choices.

Right now is all you have

We live in a 'now' society. We want everything and we want it now. Money, a big house, a luxury car, everything that the world presents as success and happiness, we want, we want it all and we believe we deserve it. Our culture screams for results today, not tomorrow, not next week, but now, today.

The challenge of fulfilling the need to have everything you want today with the demands of looking towards your future in order to bring about success and happiness is unavoidable.

When this is the situation, the best thing to do is turn to that great theory from economics – delayed gratification. This involves making tough decisions today, which might mean putting off the easy and pleasurable things now to have a more meaningful and successful future. It means having the ability to forgo an immediate pleasure or reward in order to gain a more substantial one later.

Living a life of self-leadership is not a 'here and now' or even a one-off event. It is about taking one step at a time. Not some massive leap, but a series of incremental steps. Small, consistent movement in the direction of where you want to bring your life and work will get you there. For many who do achieve success and happiness, it is about being an overnight success that was twenty years in the making. One small step after the other will radically alter the direction of your life over time. If pursued, success and happiness will demand determination, patience, persistence and courage – all traits of the self-leader.

Where You Are Now

Self-leaders know where they are going so the decisions they make are always taking them in the right direction. The most powerful motivator in the world is having a purpose. With this in mind:

- They let their vision serve as a lighthouse, lighting the path that must be followed, amid the confusion and hassle that may, and often will, surround them.

- Self-leaders live the vision rather than just have it written down on a piece of paper or saved on a computer.

- If they are in a relationship or have a family, they look to see how they can engage with their partner or family and make the vision a reality with their support and assistance.

- Self-leaders understand that once they have a vision for their future, there is a need to constantly check it against the present state of their life.

- Regardless of what comes their way, they work at cherishing the vision. They let it be the road map of what they ultimately want to achieve in their life.

Once they know their vision, decisions can become easier to make and self-leaders will know the reasons behind what they need to get done. They realise and accept that past accomplishments are no guarantee of future success and happiness. By the same token, past failures will not prevent them from creating their own future of success and happiness.

Congratulations! You have now taken the fourth step on the path of self-leadership. As you progress along the path, remember to:

- Set out a vision for the life you want to live

- Believe in your vision

- Accept that you are worthy of reaching it

TRAIT 5
KNOWING YOUR MISSION

The secret of getting ahead is getting started. The secret of getting started is breaking your complex overwhelming tasks into small manageable tasks, and then starting on the first one.

Mark Twain

Self-leaders know that having a vision means more than bringing their life and work to a successful, happy place. It is as much about how they get there.

This is why it is vital to have a personal mission statement that supports the vision they want to achieve. When there is an understanding of where they want to go with their life and work, and how they want to get there, then it is possible to review and recommit to it frequently. When you have a real and genuine sense of ownership over how it is you are going to achieve your vision, you will be more upbeat and enthusiastic about the journey ahead.

The most effective way to achieve what you have set out to do is to develop a personal mission statement. This focuses on what you want to be and the values or principles you want to follow in pursuit of your vision. The mission statement itself might be very short, perhaps not more than a sentence or paragraph. But development of the mission statement should grow out of deep introspection and a great deal of reflection.

In a short and distinct way, the mission statement needs to answer the following question: "How will you live as a person as you move forward to reach the vision you have for your life and work?"

> It is better to follow your own life's mission, however imperfectly, than to assume the life mission of another person, however successfully.
>
> *The Bhaghavad Gita*

A personal mission statement based on good principles will set out the way you want to live your life and the standards you aspire to live by. It can serve as a personal constitution or charter, as the foundation for making major life and work decisions. It will help you build a firm grounding on which to achieve your vision for the future, and remind you how you will get there. Having a written mission statement will give you a focus, keep you on track or get you back on track if you do stray.

A mission statement has these positive effects:

- It will act as a great mechanism for your long-term development as a person.

- It will support you in everyday decision-making.

- It will motivate and arouse positive emotion.

Having a written mission statement will provide a focus and keep you pointed in the right direction, reminding you where it is you want to get to and how it is you want to get there. It will allow you to flow with changes. For instance, you may have a vision to live by the sea (your vision). This will take hard work, a lot of saving and living with a principle of delayed gratification (your mission). So your mission is to travel to your vision by working hard, saving and delaying gratification (rather than moving in and marrying a woman/man – who already lives by the sea – whom you don't love). Having your mission statement written down allows you to look at it regularly and make any necessary changes and improvements as you grow and develop both personally and professionally.

The Mission Statement

Exercise

In a very clear and concise way, your mission statement needs to answer the following question, as it will set out how it is you are going to live your life as you move towards reaching your vision. It needs to be able to exert a powerful influence on your day-to-day actions as you live out your life.

How will you live as a person in order to reach your vision? Having reviewed your vision, choose four or five words or phrases that best describe you or how you would like to be described as you move forward in pursuit of your vision.

Some examples are: calm / challenging / positive / determined / upbeat / trusting / with self-belief / total confidence / inner knowing / in partnership / with good humour / driven / through continuous learning

Now take your four or five words and/or phrases that say how best you would like to move forward and achieve your vision. Then turn them into two (or three, maximum) succinct sentences.

Having done this, leave it for a day, then review it and see if anything needs to be added or taken away.

Make the necessary changes and see if it clearly states how you want to achieve your vision. If you need to make any changes, you should do so.

This is now your mission statement.

This is how you would like to achieve your vision.

This is how you want to travel in pursuit of your vision.

This is the mission statement I live by in pursuit of my life's vision:

My mission is to pursue my life's vision in the belief that everything is going to work out just right and that I am truly good enough to do so.

Brother Martin is a monk who has chosen to live and work in some of the most marginalised and disadvantaged communities both in Ireland and in other parts of the world. He is a dedicated life learner but also a person of action. His life of action is one that involves being there for others, in a quiet and unassuming way.

He dedicates his life to supporting others to grow and develop to their full potential.

Br. Martin strives to be truly present to those with whom he comes into contact, either personally or professionally, so he can help them achieve their full potential here on this earth. (This is the vision I believe he is working from.) Now how does he do this? This is his mission: To live a simple lifestyle with personal honesty and integrity and at all times strive to be true to himself.

SETTING MEANINGFUL GOALS

Man is a goal-seeking animal. His life only has meaning if he is reaching out and striving for his goals.

Aristotle

> If your **vision** is a desired future place that you want to get to and your **mission** is how you intend travelling there, then your **goals** are the results you will have to achieve if you are to live out your mission and reach your vision.

Let's go back to Andrew who we came across in Trait 4: Having a Vision for your Life and Work.

In the first instance, we worked together and agreed where his life was really at:

1. He was in a bit of a rut. He'd get up in the morning and go to work. He had a permanent job that was enjoyable but no longer proved in any way challenging to him.

2. Having come home in the evenings, he might play his saxophone (he was quite musical but had never pursued it in any meaningful manner), watch television and then go to bed.

3. This routine really only changed at weekends when he might go to a match with his friends and then for a few drinks. He wasn't in a relationship and hadn't been for some time.

Having agreed where his life was at, we set out his vision:

To have a life that is enjoyable and fulfilling, both personally and professionally.

Now how was he to achieve this vision in a practical manner so as to have it become a reality? He set himself the following four goals in pursuit of his vision:

1. To stay in his job as this was something he enjoyed, and with the achievement of goal 2 he believed he would then find new challenges within it.

2. To complete an evening course in accountancy (something he always had an interest in) as this would also open up new challenges within his work. (This might also be a good way to meet women as he was not in a relationship.)

3. To get saxophone lessons.

4. To play in a band. (This, too, might be a good way to meet women but would also get him out of the house in the evening and give him something to do at weekends in addition to what he was already doing.)

These four things (staying in his job, pursuing an evening course, getting saxophone lessons and playing in a band) he believed could lead to the following:

- Having a more enjoyable and fulfilling working life. The evening course would lead to personal and professional growth.

- Getting to live a more enjoyable life outside of work as he would now get to pursue his interest of playing the saxophone and have the opportunity to play in a band, helping to broaden his social circle.

- Starting a relationship.

He now had a vision for his life and work as well as a way to see it become a reality that he was both prepared and determined to invest time, effort, energy and financial resources in to make it happen.

Goal setting can often seem like an easy thing to do, but you need to spend time coming up with the goals you would like to see achieved in pursuit of your life's vision. Decisions need to be made when setting goals – as you select one goal, it might mean having to overlook other aspects of your life.

For many people setting out their vision and living the six traits of the self-leader to achieve it, the goal-setting process is the hardest part, as they have to state very clearly what they do and do not want to do in the future.

Having meaningful goals changes you because it forces you to think through priorities and align behaviour with beliefs in pursuit of your vision. Having goals will lead to other people seeing that you are not being driven by what is happening around you – they will start to see that you are in control and responding, not just reacting, in pursuit of the life you want to live. These goals will give you a sense of knowing how you want to bring your life forward and this will be exciting.

When setting your meaningful goals, you are aiming to create, shape and nurture a clear way to achieve your vision.

Goals give structure, clarity and direction to your vision. They keep you focused on long, intermediate and short-term targets towards which your time and energy need to be directed if the vision is to be achieved. Living a life of self-leadership is all about designing a desired future and identifying ways to bring it about. Defining your goals is the best way to show you how to get there. It is essential to put in place a set of goals that will help you reach your vision. When the goals are meaningful, well thought out and have a realistic chance of being achieved, you will be very satisfied once they have been accomplished.

Once you have set the goals, you need to refine them repeatedly until you are left with only a small number of very significant goals that you can focus on to see the vision realised. As you do this, you need to make sure the goals you have set are ones you genuinely want to achieve in pursuit of the life you want to live. When the significant goals have been selected, set a series of small goals that will build up to these larger ones. Keeping goals small, incremental and manageable in pursuit of the significant ones will give you more opportunities for reward.

Having personal goals means getting down to practicalities and stating what must be done to achieve your life's vision.

Goals that are too easy or too hard can have an adverse effect on motivation. Having both short and long-term goals will help alleviate any feelings of frustration and disappointment you might have if the short-term ones are not achieved within the timeframe you have set for them.

For a goal to be effective, it needs to focus on results rather than activity. The goals need to help you identify where you want to be and know when you have arrived. They should bring together your efforts and energy and give meaning and purpose to all you do. You should be able to convert the goals into your daily activities so you can be proactive in achieving them. If they are set out in such a way as to allow you to take charge of your life, you can then make the things happen that will enable you to reach your personal vision. Having clear goals will keep you focused on what you want to achieve.

> French poet and playwright, Victor Hugo, emphasised the importance of having a firm plan for one's life: "He who every morning plans the transactions of the day and follows out that plan carries a thread that will guide him through the labyrinth of the most busy life." When you set out your goals in pursuit of achieving your vision, you, too, are setting out the transactions of your day and life and this will help you stay focused on getting done that which must be done.

Achieving Your Goals

The easiest and simplest way to achieve your goals is to make sure they are:

1. Precise and measurable

Precise and measurable goals give a yardstick for gauging progress. When it comes to setting goals, you need to be precise, in other words have accurate, detailed and specific expected outcomes so you can measure achievement. When you do this, you'll know exactly when you have achieved the goal and can take complete satisfaction from having achieved it. This, in turn, will keep you motivated to achieve other goals.

2. Personally challenging, but realistic

A goal is something that challenges you to grow and use your potential to its fullest. It's fine if, when you establish the goal, you don't know exactly how it will be achieved. This is of the utmost importance. When setting your vision, you have to establish the destination regardless of knowing how you are going to get there. However, you often have to set the goal without knowing how you are going to achieve it.

3. Achievable within a specific time period

Attaching a date to goals creates a sense of urgency that puts the power and drive behind your daily and weekly actions to achieve it. A goal without a date by which it is to be achieved, is just a dream.

Always state each goal as a positive statement, for instance refer to owning your own home, as opposed to having a house with a twenty-five-year mortgage around your neck.

While moving in the direction of achieving goals, there is a need to check daily to ensure you are taking the right action(s) to see these goals implemented. Reviewing them regularly is also a great way of reminding yourself of the progress made and what is now most important to you.

> When faced with cancer, my friend and cousin, Kevin, had to put his life on hold and use all his energy to deal with this life-threatening illness.
>
> Kevin had a vision for his own life and that of his young family. It was a vision full of energy and enthusiasm and one he would have been happy to pursue for the rest of his life. This vision was thrown into disarray when he was faced with the challenge of undergoing treatment for cancer.
>
> Having cancer changed Kevin's life since he was no longer able to work in the job he had nor do the activities he used to do. During his treatment, he took the time to review his life and devised a new life's vision. This was also a vision full of energy and enthusiasm and one he is happy to pursue for the rest of his life.
>
> He set himself the following goals in pursuit of this vision:

> Deal with and overcome the cancer successfully.
>
> Go back to college and study again.
>
> Secure a job in his chosen field of study.
>
> Take up a hobby that all of his young family could be involved in. Having been a keen golfer before, his goal was to take up sailing instead.
>
> One of his goals was to go back to college and study again.
>
> He could have either gone or not gone back to college to study so the goal was precise and measurable.
>
> He would either finish the course of study or not so it would be personally challenging, but realistic if it was to be achieved.
>
> This would be done by a certain date – application submitted, admitted (to the course) or not, and course completed or not – so he specified a time period in which it ought to be all finished.
>
> Each of the above might well have needed to be broken down to see it all done successfully, for instance what type of course, which university, over what period of time.

If you are prepared to spend the time and put in the effort, it is possible to set clearly defined, meaningful goals.

Once you have clearly defined goals, you can easily measure and take pride in achieving them. Thus, it is possible to see progress in what might otherwise seem like a long and, at times, unachievable journey towards your vision. No matter how daunting the vision may seem, when you approach it with a positive attitude and know the goals that have to be completed for its realisation, you can achieve things that you had previously thought impossible.

Failing to meet goals does not matter too much, as long as you learn from the experience. Goals can change over time as you go forward in pursuit of the vision. Take time and adjust your goals regularly to reflect the growth in your knowledge and experience.

When you set out goals and put them down on paper, they will become clear and will build accountability and responsibility, and release positive energy. This will help you achieve and accomplish your vision.

When setting goals, it is important not to become too concerned with how they will be achieved. Stay committed, be patient and do the work that needs to be done, and then you will achieve them. Goals will become a set of actions that will have to be done and, if completed successfully, your vision will be realised.

Only three per cent of people have written goals and only one per cent review these written goals daily. While it will take time, dedication and commitment, it is possible to be in the one per cent. So get your goals written down.

Exercise

Do you believe people must have goals in life to be successful? Do the people you know who are successful have goals? If so, do they have them written down? Why don't you just go and ask them? You might be surprised at how open they will be and, in fact, they might genuinely welcome the opportunity to discuss their goals with you.

What do you think stops people from having goals in life? Is it that they are afraid of setting them and feeling bad if they don't achieve them? Or is it that they have enough to do without taking the time to set goals? Maybe they think it's something for other people to do and not them.

Perhaps they don't feel worthy of success in their lives so don't see any point in setting goals.

So what is stopping you from having goals in your life? Why do some people reach their goals and others don't? Is it because they are lucky? Is it because they are prepared to work harder than everyone else to achieve them? Is it because they are not willing to give up on what it is they believe in and want to achieve in their lives.

So what do you believe will make you achieve your goals?

Without clear goals, ambition or firm direction, the tendency will be to spend too much time doing small, easy tasks, leaving insufficient time and energy for the larger, more difficult and perhaps more important projects. Remember, when you set your goals, you build up your self-image. You see yourself as worthy of these goals and begin to develop the traits and personality that will allow you to achieve them. Knowing what you want to achieve makes it clear what to concentrate on and improve on, and often you then subconsciously prioritise that goal. Your goals will also motivate you in the short term and focus your attention on achieving what you have set out to do.

Self-leaders learn to differentiate between what is important and what is absolutely crucial. This is what you must do, too, when setting your goals: identify what is crucial and not just what is important. This means prioritising your goals and what it is you must achieve to reach your vision. It might be crucial for one person to leave their job and set up their own business if they are to achieve their vision. At the same time, it might be important to them – but not crucial – that they get to travel while carrying out their business activities.

Yet, they might have very clear goals in both areas.

Once you have created your life's vision, there is a need to identify the significant goals that you will have to achieve to see this life become a reality.

In pursuit of my life's vision, I have goals in all of the following areas:

1. Relationships/friendships and people I want to spend my time with

2. Hobbies and passions

3. Developing a personal practice, at the spiritual, physical and psychological level

4. Wealth and finance

5. Making a contribution to the world both personally and professionally – leaving a legacy

As already mentioned, once you have set your significant goals, you then need to break them down into smaller ones. These smaller goals will have to be achieved to see the significant goals realised in pursuit of your vision.

One of my significant goals relates to hobbies and passions. One of my passions is to look at and see how it is we can live a more successful and happier life. This is what led to the specific goal of writing this book.

Goal – write a book on living a successful and happy life.

To get to the point of having this book finished, so many other smaller goals needed to be agreed on and achieved.

These are the smaller goals to be met during the process of writing the book:

1. Research the topic.
2. Write an article.
3. Get feedback.
4. Do more research as the goal became to turn the article into a book, having received very positive feedback on the article.
5. Take the research and turn it into a manuscript.
6. Decide on the title/the number of words to be written/the chapter structures.
7. Get initial feedback from potential readers.
8. Incorporate the feedback where appropriate.
9. Have it edited.
10. Incorporate editor's feedback where appropriate.
11. Have the final manuscript proofread.
12. Incorporate the feedback where appropriate.
13. Get the cover designed.
14. Choose a publisher.
15. Have the book published.

Now take the vision you have created for your life and look at your mission statement. Identify the meaningful goals that you will have to achieve to see the life you wish for realised.

Then break these goals down into smaller more manageable ones to achieve your vision.

Are the goals you have now set:

- Precise and measurable?

- Personally challenging, but realistic?

- Achievable in a specific time period?

Once you have set your goals, you need to highlight your strengths and weaknesses and what part they will play in achieving your goals. Review your goals and the activities to be carried out in order to see them accomplished. Having identified the activities to be carried out, list the following:

1. What activities will you be strong at?

2. What activities will you be weak at?

Having identified what you will be strong at doing, the challenge is to then focus as much of your energy and time as possible on carrying out these activities.

As soon as you are able to, stop doing the activities you are weak at, if this is feasible, or see whether you can build relationships with and/or buy in the services of others to carry out these activities for you.

The goals that you have now set will be the transformation you seek as you move from your present situation to a far better one for you and everyone with whom you come into contact. If along the way you learn something that would lead to you changing your goals, there is a need to do so while keeping your vision at the forefront. If you notice a shortfall in your skills despite achieving a goal, you need to decide how best to move forward in pursuit of your next goal. This might mean looking to see how best to play to your strengths and minimise your weaknesses (as outlined in Trait 3: Playing to your Strengths) as you achieve your next goal(s).

Virtually any goal can be attained, if you plan the action(s) to be taken wisely and establish a realistic timeframe that makes this possible. Goals that may have previously seemed far away and out of reach eventually move closer and become attainable, not because the goals shrink but because you have grown and expanded to match them.

Where You Are Now

Goals can change over time as you move forward in pursuit of your vision. Take the time to adjust your goals regularly to reflect the growth in your knowledge and experience.

As already mentioned and to emphasise this once again, when you set your goals and get them written down, they become clear, building accountability and responsibility, as well as releasing positive energy. This, in turn, will help you achieve these goals and accomplish your vision.

When you achieve a goal, it is important to take the time to enjoy the satisfaction of having done so. Absorb the implications of meeting the goal and observe the progress that has been made towards other goals and your vision. With the experience of having accomplished a goal, review your vision, your mission and the rest of the goals to be achieved.

If you attained the goal too easily, make the next goal that bit harder. If the goal took a dispiriting length of time to achieve, then make the next goal a little easier.

Congratulations! You have now taken the fifth step on the path of self-leadership. As you progress along the path, remember to:

- Write your mission statement, saying how it is you want to achieve your vision

- Set meaningful goals to see your vision become a reality

TRAIT 6
STAYING FOCUSED

He conquers who endures.

Persius – Roman satirist

Whenever I think about being focused in life and work, the psychologist Frank Shaughnessy comes to mind.

Having obtained two first-class honours degrees from very prestigious universities, he was very 'successful'.

But he was not at all happy. He had arranged and lived his life in the belief that this attainment of education would bring him success and happiness. After accepting that this was not the case, he realised it was time to move on with his life.

Initially, this still involved further education and the pursuit of knowledge. This time, it was in the area of psychology, with a focus on studying and understanding happiness. Having completed his studies and qualified as a psychologist, he had a greater understanding of what makes him and other people happy.

As a psychologist, his life and work are now focused on working with both individuals and groups to share his knowledge and insights into happiness. His life is all about concentrating on his own happiness and that of others. He is able to show others how they, too, can focus on being happy, regardless of the circumstances they may find themselves in.

Working through the ups and downs of life and never giving in, Frank discovered what was most important to him and focused on this as his way of living and making a living.

His focus is as strong today as it was when we first met seven years ago.

The word 'focus' has two main meanings. It can refer either to the ability to sort through many issues and recognise which are most important to you: so, being able to focus deeply means being able to process things thoroughly. 'Focus' can also mean the ability to bring constant weight to bear on the issues needing attention, once they have been identified. This is the decisive-like quality of focus. When self-leaders use the word 'focus', they are incorporating both of these meanings.

The man who chases two rabbits catches neither.

Confucius

People often need to sharpen both aspects of their focus.

They have to process things thoroughly, allowing them to be decisive and thereby enabling them to manage, lead and perform with extreme accuracy and impact.

Staying focused is really about making sure you don't get pulled in every direction, only in the direction that matters most to you. This very much comes down to what you focus on. If you focus on what's good about your day, you will have a good day; when you focus on what's bad, there's a greater chance you will have a bad day. Similarly, if you focus on a problem, the problem increases; if you are prepared to focus on a solution, the solution becomes more important.

The focus is not right if we always react to and attend to what is urgent and ignore the most important things. For instance, it is important to have a pension plan but often not urgent. You might not need it now but if you keep putting it off, then one day it will become urgent or it will be too late. When we are reacting to and getting done what is urgent, it is often in response to what others have identified as urgent. Staying focused will allow you to see what is important and must be responded to in order to get that done in a timely fashion.

Meanwhile, allegedly urgent matters, if always reacted to immediately, have a greater chance of stopping you getting more important things done.

One of the simple truths of life is that people who try to do everything often achieve nothing. They often achieve nothing because they are so busy trying to do too much. By staying focused, you will put in motion a course of action that will allow you to create your unique vision and work out the best way to see it become a reality. When you do this, you have a far greater chance of achieving what is most important.

Focusing on Your Vision

Having set out your vision, written your mission statement and identified the goals that you want to achieve, you now know where to focus your attention. With this focus, you will have the greatest of clarity and direction, allowing you to be completely positive, resourceful and resilient. These are all qualities that will need to be called upon if you want to live a life of self-leadership.

This focus, this willingness to apply disproportionate pressure in pursuit of a few selected goals in life and work, won't leave you weak and limited, or even shallow, as some might claim. Counter-intuitively, this kind of unequal focus actually increases your capacity and fuels your strength.

All too often, thoughts can be cluttered and confused.

Staying focused is a great antidote to dealing with cluttered and confused thinking. There may be a lack of ability to identify the right choice and decision to be made, along with the course of action to be taken. When focused, you can more often than not cut through this maze of confusion and uncertainty. Staying focused enables you to gather and process the information required, positioning you better to make clearer decisions and take the right course of action to move you forward in life.

When you stay focused, there is much less chance of being swayed by inner doubts or external doubting voices.

If you are of 'one mind', your energies and resources are targeted in a single direction. When you take focused action in pursuit of what is most important to you, even your worst habits or personality traits will be overcome, allowing you to continue moving forward.

Achieving more success and happiness in life and work is not just a matter of getting things done but getting the right things done. What will make this possible is staying focused on what needs to get done. This will also improve as you grow and develop as a person; you will gain the experience to focus on doing the right things to reach your vision.

> Those who are living a life of self-leadership all have a great sense of focus. They are focused on what they want to achieve and the life they want to live.

If you practise getting focused, it becomes easier.

Commitment and perseverance are essential here: the more you persevere and stay committed to having focus in your life, the easier it will become and the greater the results will be. It will be a challenge to stay committed and to persevere at times, yet the more you do it, the stronger you become as a person. If you are to move forward and attain what you want, then you will need this focus to take the right action at the right time.

Knowing when to say yes and when to say no

Focusing on your vision will mean that when you say yes to something, you will also be saying no to something else. By having a clear focus, you will better understand the tradeoffs you are making based on your yes and no decisions.

When you feel better about these yes and no decisions, you have less stress. It is true that something else is not getting done, but this is now known and accepted because it is not something that is a high priority, based on the life you want to live.

People who lack a clear focus rarely accomplish what they have set out to do. They often say yes to things that don't bring them any closer to what they want to achieve.

They can often be disappointed that, as time goes on, they are no closer to where they want to be. Unfortunately, what they don't realise is that it might just be that they have been working to someone else's focus, to the detriment of their own.

Life, and all the demands placed on people to be available and contactable at all times, can often mean a great deal of pressure to run around and become distracted from doing what is important. Staying focused will keep you from getting distracted and pulled in every direction, and losing your way.

You make better decisions on how best to use your time when there is a clear focus. Having identified what to focus on, constantly remind yourself what the focus is. By maintaining focus, you will get more done and, more importantly, you will get the right things done faster. At times, you may need to accept that it's often not about getting more done, but about getting the right things done, those that will bring you forward.

Having been married for five years, Matthew and Patricia felt their lives, both personally and professionally, were being pulled in every direction, affecting their relationship and health.

They both had demanding jobs that involved travel, and different social interests. They were becoming ships that pass in the night and were no longer prepared to live that way. They wanted a different focus and were ready to commit to it.

When they consulted me, we first looked at the travelling. They both enjoyed it, so they started to coordinate their travel and only said yes to dates that matched each other's trips. They had to be strong about this and, at the same time, be smart when dealing with their respective bosses. They focused on being away at the same time so one wasn't at home alone while the other was away. They travelled together whenever possible so they could combine a break with their work. It was also cheaper as one of them was paid to travel.

They chose a hobby they could both pursue and decided to buy a bigger house that they would enjoy renovating together. While doing this, they said yes to tasks that they both enjoyed, such as painting and decorating and no to tasks that only one of them enjoyed, such as doing the garden (choosing to outsource that).

Thus, they were able to spend more time together, which has had great benefits for them both as individuals and as a couple.

Weekly Planning

If weekly planning is not already part of your life, an example has been included to show how it can be used as a great way to bring focus and a sense of action to your life on a daily and weekly basis.

Weekly planning means taking a few minutes to look at the week ahead, diarising the actions you want to achieve to move you closer to your vision. This means standing back from the week and looking at what, if anything, needs to be changed in pursuit of your vision.

The best way to stay on track in pursuit of what you want is to organise your life on a weekly basis. You can still make changes on a daily basis – some things happen that have to be dealt with as they arise. By planning for the week ahead, you are taking control over what you want to get done and how these tasks might get done.

Each week, set aside ten to fifteen minutes for reviewing your vision and what needs to be done in the coming week in pursuit of it. Personally, I find Sunday evening a good time to do this. The weekend is coming to a close, things are a little quieter and it does lead to having a sense of knowing that I'm starting the week with some control over it.

The following simple actions work for me:

1. I look at my vision and mission statements. This keeps me focused on what things I can do the following week, regardless of how big or small.

2. I review the previous week to see if I completed everything that I had set out to do.

3. I schedule in activities or tasks to be completed for the week ahead, including time to celebrate the victories or achievements of the previous week.

These three simple actions work for me. When you set weekly actions or tasks to be completed, they bring you closer to achieving your goals, which, in turn, will advance you in the direction of the future you want.

By writing weekly goals into your schedule, you will have a better chance of seeing them through. Doing this will also help you to do the following:

- See a way through the confusion and home in on the issues, realities or occurrences that will really matter during the week.

- See what you want to achieve during the week and how this can be done.

- Have a direction for the decisions you need to make and how best to make them for the week ahead.

- Have guidelines for what you should or shouldn't be doing.

> **EXERCISE**
>
> Take some time now to identify what the benefits would be to you of planning on a weekly basis. Once you have done this, decide on the most suitable time during the week to do your planning.

This is how the weekly planning system works for me: On a Sunday evening, I open up the file on my computer showing my vision and mission statements and the goals to be achieved. I then open up my diary for the week ahead to see where the activities or tasks to be achieved in pursuit of my goals can be slotted into the diary.

> **EXAMPLE**
>
> It was brought to my attention on the previous Friday before finishing work that an organisation I work with would be having a lunchtime Pilates class every week, starting on the following Thursday. As I sat on the Sunday night doing my review for the week ahead, it became clear that I would not be available for the class (much as I would have loved to go, since it is one of my goals to work on my health and fitness) because I had arranged a meeting for lunchtime on that day.
>
> Thinking about it, I realised it should be possible to move the lunchtime meeting to the Friday if I made a phone call first thing on Monday morning – that might just be enough notice for all concerned to rearrange the meeting.

VISION: To have the necessary resources to live a healthy lifestyle, doing work that I enjoy, using my strengths and allowing me to travel both personally and professionally.

MISSION STATEMENT: To pursue my life's vision in the belief that everything is going to work out just right and that I am truly good enough to do so.

GOALS: For the sake of simplicity, let's take three of the goals in pursuit of my vision:

1. Do up house, to include fixing the front door, painting the house inside and out, putting in a new bathroom, laying new carpets and cleaning up the garden.

    A) Fix front door one evening / Tuesday evening

    B) Paint living room

    C) Do garden

2. Get fit and healthy

    A) Join a gym

    B) Take up a Pilates class

    C) Eat better

3. Enjoy my work more

    A) Join one of the work clubs or societies

    B) Attend the monthly lunchtime work presentations

DIARY FOR THE WEEK

MONDAY 9am: Ring to change the lunchtime meeting on Thursday to the Friday if possible

TUESDAY Evening: Fix front door

WEDNESDAY

THURSDAY 1:00 pm: Meet client for lunch or take up a Pilates class (Having made the call first thing Monday, it proved to be possible to change the lunchtime meeting and sign up for the class.)

FRIDAY 1:00 pm: Meet client for lunch (This was rearranged the previous Monday and confirmed.)

Separate the important things from those that are urgent and allow significant time for doing both. For instance, taking up a Pilates class is important to me but it is not urgent in the sense that if I don't do it this week, it can always be done next week! By not prioritising and not getting done what is most important, there is a real danger that everything will be treated as equal. The message you are sending out then is that it doesn't really matter what does or doesn't get done. You want to accomplish what brings you forward in life and work.

There will be a far greater chance of attaining success and happiness if you have a prioritised to-do list for each day.

Once you have this, the challenge is to go further and work your way through it. This means you get to have a repeated sense of accomplishment which, in turn, will drive you on; it will build momentum and keep moving you forward.

Those who have great success and happiness in their life and work stay focused on what is most important to them as a person. Self-leaders focus on what it is they must do to move forward in life and with their work. The opposite often applies to those who have limited success and happiness as, for the most part, they become distracted and don't stay focused on what is most important to them.

Knowing what you want to achieve and staying focused will push you to take much more action to accomplish what is important to you rather than what is important to others. It is essential before taking any action in pursuit of your vision to ask yourself: "Are the actions I am taking right now consistent with my vision and the goals that I have set to achieve it?" This is a useful way to consider decisions that will affect the realisation of your vision and what it is you need to stay focused on.

Without a doubt, time invested in drawing up a vision for your life and getting focused will pay ten times over because you will be so much more efficient and effective in achieving the important things on a daily and weekly basis. The key is to stay focused on what you want to accomplish today, putting energy into taking the necessary steps to ensure you do this.

While you may have gut feelings and/or thoughts, these must be translated into action if you want to be successful.

You can answer all the questions in this book and do all the reading you like but, as the great nineteenth-century thinker, Thomas Henry Huxley, said: "The great end of life is not knowledge but action." So gather up as much information and knowledge as possible, learn from it and then focus on the action that needs to be taken to move your life forward.

Then and only then will you see successes and happiness in your life like you've never experienced before.

Self-leaders understand that you can only achieve your vision by taking action. They focus on a few actions to take them forward in life. They then take these actions – more often than not in the face of fear and the unknown. Self-leaders are always focusing on how it is they can move forward in life and with their work. The opposite is often the case for those who have limited success and happiness as, more often than not, they just stay still, rarely moving beyond their comfort zone.

COMPROMISE AND BALANCE ARE NOT ALWAYS THE ANSWER

When having to work and deal with others in life, compromise might not always be the answer if you are to stay focused on successfully realising your vision.

Equally, success and happiness often come most readily to those who reject balance in pursuit of what is most important to them. As a self-leader, at times you will have to focus on and pursue approaches that are intentionally unbalanced.

Look at those who have had the greatest 'success' in life: people like Nelson Mandela, Mother Teresa, Ryanair's Michael O'Leary and Eddie Jordan (when he was running his Formula One team) – none of whom did or do seem to live lives of balance.

> Balance is, in fact, truly overrated.

Do you really want equal amounts of time and energy to go into the most important areas of your life as well as into those of less importance? At times, you will have to be 'unbalanced' with your time and commitments. At times, you might have to decide that some areas of life and activities are more important than others. You might have to decide to put your energy and focus into what is most important to you, and this will come at the expense of other areas of your life. For instance, I have recently been invited to undertake a PhD. If I accept the invitation, I really can't see how my life will be balanced over the next three years while it is completed.

It will mean not being able to travel as much as I would like, nor spend as much time pursuing my other interests, such as sailing.

Where You Are Now

It is only by looking at where you would like to be in the future that there is any real chance of shaping this future. Looking to the future then working out where you would like to be and how this can be done is a brave thing to do. To succeed in the future, you will need to create it. The challenge is to stop postponing your hopes and dreams for another day.

Invest the time and energy in determining your focus. Be mindful of this focus each and every day, in the same way as people who are already successful and happy. If they can do it, so can you. Put the time, effort and energy into creating and maintaining a focus on what is most important to you, as well as staying focused on what will move you closer to the success and happiness you want to achieve. Focus on what you want to spend your time doing and not what someone else wants. Stop thinking about the success and happiness of others, or what they see as success and happiness for you, and start focusing on your own life's vision of success and happiness.

When the focus is crystal clear, it makes you take more action to accomplish the important things. This, in turn, helps you to accomplish more of what needs to be done. Many people believe that God laughs when they make a plan to move forward and take action within their own lives. Yes, God often does laugh when the plan is not the right one for someone. Yet, when it is the right one, then God laughs, too, but in this instance it is about getting right behind the person as they set out to see the action successfully implemented in order to live the life they want.

Congratulations! You have now taken the sixth and final step on the path of self-leadership. As you progress along the path, remember to:

- Focus on the life you want to live

- Take the necessary action to see it become a reality

Conclusion

Begin at the beginning and go on till
you come to the end; then stop.

Lewis Carroll

There is an Irish joke about a man who is lost in the countryside asking a local the way to his destination and being told, "Oh, if you want to get there, I wouldn't start from here!" That is often how it feels to us – that we should be starting from somewhere else. We may think, "If only I wasn't so young/old", "If I only had more money", "If I only had more connections in this or that industry", "If I wasn't married", "If I didn't have children" and so on.

The fact is, you have brought yourself to where you are and this is your ideal starting point. Your life today is the result of your choices and actions up to this point. There is a much better chance of you taking the right action in the future by accepting where you are right now.

There seems to be a general perception that things are bad in the world right now. But how bad are things really? Things are not as bad as they may seem as there has, in fact, never been a better time to be alive. The average person is wealthier, healthier, smarter, cleaner, safer, fitter, stronger, better informed, more peaceful, kinder, freer, more equal and happier than at any time in human history.

Self-leaders understand the concept that a boat is off track a lot of the time but, as long as it keeps coming back to the sailing plan, it will arrive at its destination. This can be true of us as individuals, families and organisations.

The key is to have an end in mind – a vision of living a life of success and happiness and a commitment to review and correct the course, in order to reach that end. There will often be the need to act like pilots and sailors who tack left and right, never assuming they can head for their destination in a straight line. At times, it may seem like you are going in the wrong direction or even backwards. Sometimes you may need to go off course or indeed backwards to stay focused on living a life of success and happiness. Just remember that a plane heading for its destination will be off course over ninety-five per cent of the time but will still get there and, for the most part, on time, if not a little early.

Now, search out and find like-minded people and kindred spirits who are looking to live a life of self-leadership if they are not already doing so. I have found and am still finding my own tribe to run with. (This is something that takes time, determination, patience and energy.) We are on the path of living out our own lives as self-leaders. Being surrounded by like-minded people will ensure you stay positive and keep you on your journey forward. Now that you are on the journey, you are living out and showing all the hallmarks of starting to live a life of success and happiness in pursuit of the vision you have for your life and work – stick at it.

Any one of the six traits, when practised with rigour, will help you increase your effectiveness as a self-leader within your life and work. Practising all six consistently will bring your life and work to where you want them to be.

By this point, you have done a lot of hard work and no doubt made some big decisions. Today you are more focused, knowing where you want to take your life, and you have set out goals that have to be achieved to lead you there. The challenge now is to continue and accelerate your progress by building on these traits and staying committed to them. This is the time to take the action to turn your good intentions into reality. You can have all the knowledge in the world but, unless you act on it, nothing will change. When feeling uncertain, choose one goal to focus on. This will give you clarity, direction and the confidence to keep going.

Never Ever Give In

> A man asked a monk he met on the path, "Which way is success?" The monk silently gestured down the path.
>
> The man was elated by the prospect that success was so close and so easy to reach, and rushed ahead.
>
> Suddenly, there came the sound 'splat'. A short while later, the man, now tattered and stunned, limped back, assuming he must have taken a wrong turn. He repeated the question to the monk, who again pointed silently in the same direction.
>
> The man nodded, turned and headed back in the same direction as before. This time, the sound of 'splat' was deafening. When the man crawled back, he was bloody, broken and angry. Screaming at the monk, he demanded to know why he was sent off in the direction of disaster. "No more pointing. Talk!"
>
> Only then did the monk speak. "Success is that way," he said. "Just a little past splat."

People often find themselves believing that when things are going badly for them, it will never end. Yet when things are going really well, they often believe it just won't last. If you do fail from time to time, there is no harm done, since failure is nothing more than learning how to win. Failure can be the avenue to success if you allow it to be. If the decisions you made in either your personal or professional life to date are making you feel like a failure, you need to reach deep inside yourself and truly believe you can still go on to live a life of success and happiness. You can learn from the decisions taken, the mistakes made and come back from the experience bigger, stronger and better prepared to move forward in life.

Developing and living out the six traits takes commitment and dedication. Everyone falters from time to time in living out these traits. The traits are simple but require consistent practice.

I personally strive to do much of what I have shared in this book and find it worthwhile and fulfilling. It gives meaning to my life and enables me to love, to serve and to try again.

Admittedly, at times, it does mean having to just hang in there, taking small steps in pursuit of living a life of self-leadership.

There will be times when you, too, will have to hang in there, adapt, change, and take calculated risks. You have to stay determined to keep moving forward in pursuit of your vision, regardless of what life throws at you.

I trust you have enjoyed reading this book and found it of practical assistance. Enjoy and celebrate every success on your journey as you move towards living the life you wish for.

What has been proposed here is not something that can be finished and done away with. It is a way of life and the challenge contained in living out the six traits will keep you striving forward for as long as you live. Accept that you are worthy of living a life of success and happiness. Now go and live the life of a self-leader and achieve this life you so wish for.

Where You Are Now

No one, not this book or even your personal coach or mentor, if you have one, can do the work for you to achieve your vision.

You must be at the point where you understand that working on yourself is a priority, that you are tired of functioning (or not functioning) as you are, that you want to thrive and not just survive in life. As you start moving in the direction of the life you want, you start to move from wishful thinking to having belief in yourself, and finally knowing what you want and how to achieve it.

As you have no doubt experienced, there is a chasm between saying and doing, a chasm that takes focus, self-discipline and not a little faith to cross if you are to go on and achieve your life's vision.

> There was a very famous actor who would go missing every afternoon for two to three hours, regardless of where they were in the shooting of the film. This caused untold hassle and expense for all involved, except for the actor himself, of course. He was so famous that the director would not even dare to ask what was going on, let alone challenge him.
>
> When filming had finished, and the atmosphere was more relaxed, the director finally did ask where the actor had been going during this time. The actor explained that his father had loved fishing and promised him that the two of them would go fishing when he retired. His father had died at fifty-four years of age, he didn't get to retire and they never had the chance to go fishing.
>
> The actor was taking no risks and went fishing every day, regardless of what was going on. The lesson the actor had learned was: Don't put off until tomorrow what you can do today.

You need to accept that, at times, you will have to embrace loss, endure pain or temporarily lose freedoms, but never give up faith and the belief in your own ability to succeed in being happy and successful in life. Remember, the path out of gloom and despair begins with you doing your best to be steadfast in taking the small actions needed to stop you giving up or surrendering to defeat. Understand that it is one thing to suffer a shocking and stunning defeat and entirely another to give up on the life you so wish to live.

Self-leadership is not only about envisioning a better future, it is also about believing in every fibre of your being, being convinced that you are the one to make this future come true. It is about the belief that you are the one to assume the responsibility for transforming the present into something better for yourself and those around you. Now please go and make it happen.

EXERCISE

The final exercise: please speak to at least one person over the next twenty-four hours and share why it is you now want to live the life of a self-leader in pursuit of having a life of success and happiness.

Once you do this, the answer will become more ingrained for you.

Thank you, take good care and God bless.

Michael E. Daly

Acknowledgements

The following people have to be acknowledged and thanked for their support and assistance in making the job of turning what started out as an article into the book you are now reading.

Thomas Hoffmann for the initial invitation to work at Nordhausen University of Applied Sciences in Germany (and Maurice Roche, too, for the wonderful hospitality he has always shown to the international guests there), leading to Dr Grazyna O'Sullivan inviting me to work at Siedce University of Natural Sciences and Humanities in Poland, and in turn Jolanta Preidiene and Lina Gaigalaite also asking me to work at Vilnius University of Applied Sciences in Lithuania and Professor María José Del Pino Espejo inviting me to work at University Pablo de Olavide in Spain. They all inspired, challenged and allowed me to dive so much more deeply into this topic while working with their universities.

Writing is a very solitary profession that makes writers face themselves on paper. It is the editor's job to bring clarity when the written words start to blur on the screen and give support throughout the process of producing the finished book. Paul Egan was there from day one to the very end. I'll be ever grateful to him for making this doable at times when it just seemed too much. Brendan Garland gave great assistance with the initial stages of this work and excellent support also throughout the whole journey. Anne McFadden and Kevin Malone took charge of pulling this book together with their insightful comments and masterful editing skills. They made the editing work an incredible experience of learning and fellowship. Finally,

Leda Sammarco and Linda Jayne Turner came in for the final edit that transformed this into the book it is. Then a host of supporters, readers and critics need to be thanked, including Professor Jim Blythe for putting everything in motion that led to my working with Nordhausen University of Applied Sciences. I'll be ever grateful to him and to the author and inspired entrepreneur, Nick Williams, for putting me on this path of discovery – we need more people like them in this world. Nick is a great friend and has always been a constant source of inspiration and encouragement.

To those who read both the original article and the book before publication, thanks for your honest and open feedback, for bringing your intelligence, insight and experience to bear.

This surely did help focus the traits and writing hugely. I am indebted to Gerry McLarnon (thanks to him, too, for the ever-ready listening ear), Declan Hogan, James Russell, Patrick Russell, David Blight, Brian Walsh, Dermot O'Rourke, James Paul Rodell, Freddie Reid, Paddy Reid, Br. Martin Byrne, Frank Shaughnessy, Marie Byrne, Martin Brocklebank, Allyson Lambert, Kate T Lawler and Brendan Daly (thanks to him, too, for the sound advice and great encouragement along the way).

Thanks must also go to Des Doherty, Gerry McDonald, James Sweetman and Kevin 'Tubby' Corraway for taking the time to meet with me and share their knowledge and insights from their professional backgrounds.

Thanks to Andy Doogue, Sharon Kennedy, Jean MacGiollariogh, John O'Hara, Helen Bee, Gerry Byrne, Sue Blythe, Amerjit and Sarah Walia and Professor Gerd Mühlenbeck for their friendship and support over the years.

Thanks to Peter Duggan, Aishling Kearney, Mark and Claire McGowan, Robbie and Sue O'Rourke, Mary Rose Curran, Ann Kelly, Frank Brennan, Niall Boland, Mairead McKenna, John Clearly, Noel Mahoney, Larry and Peggy Meany, Matthew and Michelle Walsh and all who have sailed on Heatwave. Thanks to Imam Ismail Kotwal. Thanks to Cathy Ryan, Helen Bohan, Carol McInerney and all involved in Five Rhythms.

I'm so very grateful to Christopher Greenaway of CGW Publishing, for his faith in me and his expertise, patience, time, and commitment to seeing the process right through to the book you are now holding in your hands or reading as an E-book.

There are times in our lives when we so need a person in our corner. Annette McGee was one such person. Thank you so much for being there.

To Lilly Daly, Pauline Malone and all of the Daly and Malone families, thank you.

About The Author

As an author, speaker and consultant on self-leadership my goal is to enable you to achieve true and real success in all areas of your life and work faster and easier than you ever thought possible.

Having finished at St. Kevin's College, Ballygall Road, Dublin, a Christian Brothers' run school I went on to study to become a member of the Irish order of Christian Brothers'. It was their commitment and dedication to enabling all those that they worked with to be the best that they could be, that inspired me to become one of the Brothers. It was there that I believed I could make my biggest impact in enabling individuals and communities to be the best that they could be.

Much of my time there was dedicated to studying, including qualifying as a Social Care Worker with the Dublin Institute of Technology. I also got to experience how with the right knowledge and expertise individuals, groups and organisations really could be enabled to achieve true and real success.

After eight years of this rewarding work and great personal growth my time came to move on from the Christian Brothers' and bring my passion, knowledge and experience to my next best level and a wider audience.

My work began initially with teenagers and young adults. This involved getting them to take responsibility for themselves and ownership of their own lives and destinies. This then led to being offered and the taking up a leadership position which involved enabling adults, committees, communities, groups and organisations to be the best that they could be in creating better futures for both themselves and all those with whom they got to work with.

After many years of this work, it was time for me to take the next brave step and move on once again. So, for the last seventeen years I have been a writer, speaker and consultant. During this time there has also been the bonus of being asked to take on leadership roles within organisations for which I had acted as a consultant. My work today along with my over thirty years' experience of working for and with individuals, groups and organisations is all about striving to be the best that I can possibly be. I'm very grateful to have got to use all this time to study, research, write about and speak to individuals, groups and organisations on self-leadership, achieving true and real success in life and work as well as living your life purpose.

This makes what I do, all about enabling those that I work for, to be the best that they can possibly be. This has and always will be at the core of the work I do – getting people to live lives of self-leadership in pursuit of living lives of true and real success.

While being based in Ireland I am regularly invited to give presentations and lead workshops internationally. I hold qualifications in Social Care, Public Administration and have an MA in Health Care Management.

For more information, contact Michael personally by e-mailing: michael@michaeldalyireland.com

To learn more about The Six Traits of Self-Leadership, visit: www.michaeldalyireland.com

www.ingramcontent.com/pod-product-compliance
Lightning Source LLC
LaVergne TN
LVHW091256080426
835510LV00007B/280